Dear Friend,

It's my great pleasure to share with you my new book titled *Preserving Multigenerational Wealth: How to Lead A Flourishing Family Enterprise.* This book is part memoir and part overview of the family office industry. It reflects a lot of the hard-earned and practical wisdom I gained from leading the Pitcairn family office over several decades. Writing it was truly a labor of love.

I hope you enjoy the book and find it both informative and beneficial to you as a family office professional.

With warmest regards,

THE EVOLUTION OF PITCAIRN:
AMPLIFYING WEALTH FOR HUMANITY

PRESERVING
MULTIGENERATIONAL
WEALTH

HOW TO LEAD
A FLOURISHING
FAMILY
ENTERPRISE

DIRK JUNGÉ

WHAT OTHERS ARE SAYING ABOUT DIRK JUNGÉ AND THIS BOOK

"This book couldn't come at a better time for the family office industry or from a more credible voice than that of Dirk Jungé. His many years working with families and family businesses have given him an unparalleled perspective, and I can't think of anyone who can more authoritatively address the subject. Working with Dirk at Pitcairn, I saw firsthand how his innovative ideas and leadership helped numerous multigenerational families. He's has been a mentor and a friend for nearly thirty years, and I have learned more from him than I can ever say. I'm delighted that a much larger audience can now benefit from his vast knowledge and experience through this important new book."

— **Leslie Voth, CEO and Chairman of Pitcairn**

"Dirk Jungé has the tendency to influence you to start seeing the positive in anything and everything you do. He has the unique gift and ability to lift up people all around him to empower them to achieve their best and most empowered lives. Dirk has many passions but always keeps his family as a top priority and treasures his family heritage and the culture for all families. He certainly gets the most out of every day and each experience. Read this book and you too will learn to live a fulfilled life and leave your legacy!"

— **Adam R. Kaufman, Founder Up2 Foundation**

"Dirk Jungé is a living legend! He is the essence of leadership, love, influence, and passion. His heart is as big as they come, and he has dedicated his life not only in service to his family, but being in service to others! Read this book and not only will you learn how to create and preserve wealth, but more importantly, how to use it to positively impact all of humanity! This book is a must add to your personal library because it is sure to become an instant classic!"

— **Patrick Snow, Publishing Coaching and International Best-Selling Author of *Creating Your Own Destiny* and *The Affluent Entrepreneur***

"Living lives intertwined with love and care for family, for employees, for friends, and for the business is an incredibly complex juggling journey that with all its ups and downs can be incredibly fulfilling as Dirk Jungé has proven by managing it so very well."

— **Ann Dugan, Founder and Assistant Dean of Institute for Entrepreneurial Excellence, University of Pittsburgh**

"Dirk served as an independent director on our board for six years. He was a constant source of encouragement, great ideas, and thoughtful questions. His service culminated in us doing a large spin-off that helped the family immeasurably. We will forever be in his debt."

— **Joe Popolo, CEO of Charles & Potomac Capital, LLC**

"Dirk Jungé is fantastic. He is an inspirational man in so many regards. He has a gratitude for life, and he capitalizes on that gratitude through action, experiences, relationships, and philanthropy. His life mission has been very poignant. I admire a great man like Dirk who as "a man in the arena" knows the taste of both defeat and victory and who endeavors to do more for family, community, country, and God."

— **Bob Campana, Venture Capitalist and Host of the Up2 Podcast Series**

"Dirk Jungé is an exemplar of a family steward. Dirk is a legacy to our industry, one that remains in an early stage of its evolution. He is a visionary and builder in transitioning Pitcairn from a single-family office to a true multi-family office, a model for our industry."

— **Jamie McLaughlin, Founder & CEO, J. H. McLaughlin & Co.**

"Dirk Jungé is an inspiring global leader in the family business world and beyond. His pioneering spirit and vision, along with his steadfast leadership, have impacted many throughout his journey. Dirk's commitment to create and preserve family legacies has been a positive and influential force in the field of family business. The culmination of his vast knowledge and rich experience is captured in this insightful book."

— **Caroline Coleman Bailey, Founder and CEO of Premier Growth and Author of *Rooted in Family: Honoring the Past While Creating Our Future***

"Mettle is the courage to carry on. If someone wants to 'test your mettle,' they want to see if you have the heart to follow through when the going gets tough. Having the mettle to do something means you have guts. In short, you're a pretty impressive person. Over the years, Dirk has clearly demonstrated his courage and resilience in his personal and professional lives. Dirk and I have worked side-by-side in the work of families of wealth and families who own businesses. I have observed Dirk draw on his breath of life experience, applying his insights to produce relevant and viable solutions. Over the years, we have shared many cigars discussing some of the thorniest issues facing family systems. Congratulations, my friend, because this book is the ultimate roadmap for other family leaders to preserve multigenerational wealth!"

— **David Bork, Family Business Consultant, Coach, and Author**

"As a member and family leader of one of the most prominent family offices in the world, as a trusted advisor to so many high net worth families, as a counselor to younger generations of families of wealth and as a leading board member of many family-owned businesses, Dirk offers unique experience, wisdom, and perspective on how to flourish as entrepreneurial families. No one I know has had so many unique experiences to share in his professional career and family life. On a more personal note, I've known this incredible man for more than forty years. I am blessed to call Dirk my best friend! As much as he can be the life of the party, he brings that same energy and encouragement to his family, friends, and all the families he has counseled over his career. He certainly lives his life to the fullest. Thanks for sharing this "how to do book" for all our benefit."

— François M. de Visscher, FODIS Founder,
Family Business Consultant and Advisor

"Dirk is special! He brings his zest to all projects, so this is a book that is special, with a wealth of stories and lessons. Dirk is an icon in the family wealth area. We are lucky to have him share so openly, and with a storyteller's flair, the history of his own family. It took decades of effort to make Pitcairn into the award-winning family office it is today. He generously shares their lessons. As an independent board member for ten years, I can vouch for his dedication to choosing the path that is best for his company's clients. Through all challenges, he is kind, caring, and respectful."

— **Barbara R. Hauser, LLC, Author and Advisor to Families of Wealth**

"In his wonderful book, Dirk Jungé takes us on his life's journey and purpose: to grow a great family; to dynamically encourage the growth of a great firm, Pitcairn; and to serve intentionally the larger community of his faith and our field of seeking to help families flourish. In all these arenas, he has been a creative builder and a dynamic preserver. He epitomizes that wealth means well-being in all of its iterations. His is a life so well worth journeying with."

— **James E. Hughes, Jr., Family Wealth Advisor and Author**

"*Preserving Multigenerational Wealth* is a revolutionary book that will inspire wealthy families to think about the legacy they want to leave to the current younger generation and to future generations. It will teach you how to get buy-in from family members and how to buy-out those no longer interested in participating in family enterprises. Even if you are not wealthy, this book will teach you much about the pros and cons of having money and how to use wealth for the wellbeing of all once you acquire it. Thank you, Dirk Jungé, for this eye-opening, well-thought-out, and generous offering that will benefit everyone who reads it."

— Tyler R. Tichelaar, PhD and Award-Winning Author of
Narrow Lives and *When Teddy Came to Town*

"Dirk Jungé's *Preserving Multigenerational Wealth* is a remarkable reflection of his unique persona. His extensive knowledge in the family office industry is impressive, but what truly sets Dirk apart is his genuine care for the financial wellbeing of all families, not just his own. His insightful exploration of wealth gaps beyond racial divides illuminates an often-overlooked facet of wealth management, demonstrating his commitment to inclusivity."

"Moreover, Dirk's fascinating life experiences and global perspectives, fueled by his extensive travels, enrich his life's work, infusing it with unique anecdotes and diverse cultural insights. His refined taste shines throughout the conversations we've shared, elevating them from mere advice to true food for thought."

"In *Preserving Multigenerational Wealth*, Dirk's expertise and genuine care coalesce into a valuable, insightful read. This book is not only a testament to his knowledge but also a shining endorsement of his character."

— Osyris Uqoezwa, Chairman of Golden Leaf Holdings

THE EVOLUTION OF PITCAIRN:
AMPLIFYING WEALTH FOR HUMANITY

PRESERVING MULTIGENERATIONAL WEALTH

HOW TO LEAD A FLOURISHING FAMILY ENTERPRISE

AVIVA
PUBLISHING
NEW YORK

DIRK JUNGÉ

PRESERVING MULTIGENERATIONAL WEALTH

How to Lead a Flourishing Family Enterprise

Published by:

Aviva Publishing
Lake Placid, NY 12946
518-523-1320
www.avivapubs.com

Dirk Jungé
(215) 327-8874
DirkJunge@icloud.com

www.PreservingMultigenerationalWealth.com
www.DirkJunge.com

ISBN #: 978-1-63618-282-7
Library of Congress #: 2023911635

Editors: Tyler Tichelaar and Larry Alexander, Superior Book Productions
Cover Designer and Interior Book Layout: Fusion Creative Works

Every attempt has been made to properly source all quotes

Printed in The United States of America

First Edition

2 4 6 8 10 12

DEDICATION

To my wife and life partner of more than fifty years, Judith A. Jungé.

To my four children, their spouses, and grandchildren who have brought me so much joy.

To my brother, Jan Jungé, who passed away prematurely fifty years ago. In my family, I was closest to him in age and emotionally. He was a super-gifted, incredible musician, artist, and athlete who also graduated at the top of his class with a degree in architecture from Carnegie Mellon Institute. After college, he was a protégé of leading Philadelphia architect Louis I. Khan. He also spent a summer with *The Beatles*. I know we will be together again at some point in the future, and his passing is all part of God's grand plan.

To all those who have mentored me and contributed to my development in life.

Finally, to you, the reader. May this book inspire you to live your best life for you and your family.

ACKNOWLEDGMENTS

I would like to extend a special thank you to the following friends, associates, mentors, and those who helped make this book possible:

Craig Aronoff, Dr. Richard Aronson, Carolyn Bailey, Ray Betler, David Bork, Richard Boylan, Dick Brickman, Deb Bright, Peter Coy, Peter Davis, Thomas Dudley Davis, Ann Dugan, Don Freeman, Susan Friedmann, Judy Green, Sara Hamilton, Barbara Hauser, Lee Hausner, Jay Hughes, James Olin Hutchinson, Dennis Jaffee, James F. Jungé, Ivan Lansberg, Jeffrey Lauderbach, Gerry Lenfest, Tom Livergood, Greg McCann, Tom McCulloch, Tom McHugh, Jamie McLaughlin, Dr. Eric Muten, Ron Nelson, Tony Odner, Ellen Perry, Ernesto Pose, Christina Rice, Clay Riddell, Jim Riddell, Marty Roark, François de Visscher, Leslie Voth, John Ward, Peter White, Kathy Wiseman, and Hans Ziegler.

I am also grateful for the professionalism and expertise of my book publishing team:

Larry Alexander, Susan Friedmann, Shiloh Schroeder, Patrick Snow, and Tyler Tichelaar.

DISCLAIMER

Even though I am a Chartered Financial Analyst (CFA), now being retired, I am no longer active in offering investment advice. This book is not meant to offer financial advice to you, your family, or your family business enterprise. Rather, it is intended to give you ideas, strategies, and techniques to encourage you to both create and preserve multigenerational wealth. Additionally, my goal is to offer perspectives on being of use to humanity while leveraging wealth as an amplifier. I encourage you to seek advice from your attorneys, financial planners, accountants, family wealth advisors, and family therapists to ensure you achieve your specific financial and life goals.

"To believe in a thing is to do something about it."

— John Pitcairn, Jr.
(*John Pitcairn: The Uncommon Entrepreneur*
by Richard R. Gladish)

CONTENTS

PART III:

PART IV:

PREFACE
A NOTE TO THE READER

"Don't wish it was easier, wish you were better.
Don't wish for less problems, wish for more skills.
Don't wish for less challenge, wish for more wisdom."

— Jim Rohn

I fully appreciate that I am part of a legacy family, and as a result, I know I am privileged. I feel fortunate to be part of the many generations of Pitcairn who trace their roots back to the Scottish emigrant, John Pitcairn, Jr. I've thought a great deal about legacy and its influence on family. I choose to see legacy as a river that flows and benefits the family. Those of the current generation are charged with protecting the source and the quality of the water for future generations. I accept this responsibility and have committed my life to this worthy cause. This book attempts to capture the evolution of the Pitcairn legacy from my viewpoint.

That being said, I hope my book, with its stories, observations, and reflections with possible advice, will be a catalyst for positive change for you, your family, and its enterprise. I trust my zest for life's experiences will encourage you to step out of your comfort zone to experience the thrill of doing something you never thought possible. And finally, I'm so grateful to all those who have influenced me and helped me to experience all of life's wonders.

I don't believe anyone should apologize for who they are or their family of origin! I am blessed, as you will read in this book, and everything my family has accomplished for more than one hundred years has been the result of commitment to hard work. As such, I am humbled and grateful for the work ethic that was instilled in me by my forefathers as a young boy. I have carried it with me throughout my lifetime. I am hopeful your family has done the same for you, but if not, perhaps my book will inspire you to develop the same commitment to hard work and to emulate and pass it down to your children and grandchildren for generations to come.

One of my favorite quotes is: "If you want it bad, you will get it bad." To me, this means if you let your emotions dictate your financial actions (including capital infusion), you will likely shortchange due diligence and the thoughtful skepticism needed for long-term positive results. Another expression that comes to mind is: "Don't ask someone to marry you on your first date." Doing so would be too soon and wouldn't bode well for the future. It is fine to be enthusiastic about a new venture, but balance that with cautious optimism—just don't fall in love too early.

My goal in writing this book is not to impress you with all my accomplishments and experiences, but rather to pass on to you and your family some habits that can become rituals for your family and, as a result, create, build, sustain, and preserve multigenerational wealth.

I encourage you to read this book, complete the exercises, and be open to the strategies offered and lessons learned from the stories told. By doing so, I believe you, too, will become the captain of your ship, the creator of your destiny, and also achieve complete freedom. I believe in you! Here's to your best days ahead and leaving a legacy behind for your family!

This book is a reflection of my years of study of families in business and families with shared wealth. My hope is you, as a member of both, will expand your view to see your shared organizations as a "family enterprise." By taking this viewpoint, you will be in a position to create and sustain multigenerational wealth. I call this "total family wealth."

My definition of a family enterprise includes the following elements, and usually appears in the second and third generations of successful family businesses:

1. A family operating business

2. A family office

3. A family council

4. Family philanthropy

5. Family trusts (sometimes a private trust company)

6. Family sensitive real estate

7. Family archives/museum/art (heritage makings)

Families are well advised to have their governance processes incorporate this more holistic view of the family and its various functions.

Leadership and successions programs should be focused on educating and developing family members to take on important leadership roles for all these enterprise elements. Perhaps the most important leadership role for family members is their preparations for becoming members of the various boards, family councils, trusteeships, and executive management.

I recommend developing a "family enterprise constitution." Make sure when developing this constitution that you factor in all five forms of capital: *financial, intellectual, human, social,* and *spiritual.*

As I like to say, "Why does this all seem so complex? Because it is!"

INTRODUCTION
INITIATING YOUR VISIONS

"Optimism is the faith that leads to achievement.
Nothing can be done without hope and confidence."

— Helen Keller

Did you know that the success of a family business from one generation to the next decreases dramatically? For example, only 13 percent of successful family businesses succeed by the third generation (G3), and by the fourth (G4), perhaps only 5 percent succeed. Hence, I share this adage: "Shirtsleeves to shirtsleeves in three generations."

This phenomenon needs further research. Whatever the numbers are, they are alarming! So much so that I have dedicated my life's work to helping family business enterprises succeed for multiple generations. Specifically, my goal is to assist family business enterprises in both creating and preserving multigenerational wealth.

Do you want this for your family business enterprise? Are you concerned about how you can help your family survive? Do you stay up nights with ulcer-producing anxiety trying to figure out how to sustain your family and its enterprise for the future? Do you worry about how to fairly deal with your inheritances, protect what you or others have created, and minimize your tax burden? Or finally, do you want to learn how to leverage your family business enterprise's wealth to amplify it to help improve our world? If any of these questions catch your attention, you have come to the right place. Hopefully, this book can help.

I understand the challenges of wealth, the internal desire to be a steward and a conduit to pass it down to future generations while protecting the core principle. I have been in your shoes. I understand the loneliness and isolation of wealth and what it can do for your perspective. I understand this so much that I decided to write this book.

In this book, you will learn how to:

- Use wealth as an amplifier
- Protect and sustain generational wealth
- Properly distribute inheritances
- Build a successful family office
- Set family and foundational values
- Invest in personal and organizational development
- Experience the benefits of being a lifelong student of leadership
- Gain a new view of defining a family legacy

This book is a compendium of stories, networks, resources, and individuals who have had a profound influence on my development over the last sixty years. It is now my honor to share this knowledge with you to benefit your family and its future.

My personal *mission statement* is to live a principled life full of accomplishment and passion in service to family, church, country, community, and the globe.

1. My primary audience consists of the consultants and advisors who serve family businesses and families of wealth.

2. My secondary audience is family leaders who find themselves at the apex of leadership or are transitioning into higher leadership positions and see their family systems (family businesses, activities, wealth, philanthropy, etc.) as a family enterprise.

3. My tertiary audience consists of coming generations of your family enterprise.

My hope is this book may help any family avoid the from shirtsleeves to shirtsleeves in three generations phenomenon. I believe my personal situation as an owner and leader of a family enterprise spanning four generations and looking to the fifth, sixth, and seventh, is helpful in aiding other family enterprises to flourish. One of my favorite quotes is by Victor Hugo: "There is nothing more powerful than an idea whose time has come."

I, of course, don't have all the answers to this complex topic, so please accept my attempt to be of service. However, I believe when you apply the strategies, techniques, wisdom, and suggestions offered here to your life and family business enterprise, you will be able to achieve what the title and subtitle of my book promises. You will be *Preserving Multigenerational Wealth* and know *How to Lead a Flourishing Family Enterprise.*

In closing, I realize memoirs sound old and stuffy, so instead of writing *The Life and Times of Dirk Jungé*, I wrote a wealth strategy book. But I still hope you will be inspired, amused, and entertained by the stories. I understand my perspective is rooted in being male, white, and privileged. Even so, I am always looking to evolve. So I find myself writing this book in my "man cave" on my property in a converted dairy barn, where I turned the bull pen into my office (surrounded by Philadelphia Eagles, 76ers, Flyers sports paraphernalia, and loving family photos). As I attempt to reflect upon and capture my life stories that might inspire you to take a leadership role in your life, family, and business, I'm smoking a nice Cuban cigar and hoping I might help you achieve your heart's desire!

PART I:

SETTING FAMILY AND FOUNDATIONAL VALUES

"Your heart was born free;
have the courage to follow it."

— William Wallace

Chapter 1

REMAINING CALM IN TIMES
OF CRISIS AND TERROR

"At any given moment you have the power to say:
'This is not how the story is going to end.'"
— Christine Mason Miller

Many people believe the ability to remain calm is a superpower. Furthermore, once you master this power of the mind, you get the opportunity to develop your single focus in times of stress and write the ending to your life's story since the pen is in your hand. I certainly believe this, especially in times of crisis when your life is on the line! As author, artist, and explorer Christine Mason Miller says above, "*This is not how the story is going to end.*"

I have experienced this mindset numerous times in my own life and business. On those occasions, I have used my single-minded focus to stay in the moment in times of stress and crisis to achieve the result I desire for my future. In one case, from the cockpit of a plane I decided, "This is not how my story is going to end" due to my ability to stay in the moment and perform, which actually saved my life as you will read later in this chapter.

Let me start this chapter by defining "calm." Then I will share with you three stories that will inspire you to do a better job at remaining calm in today's world full of chaos and uncertainty! My story below prevented a catastrophic plane crash of a Piper Super Cub I was piloting in front of my father, whom I deeply loved and respected, as he sat on the deck of the fishing lodge with cocktail in hand watching my aerobatics over a pristine bay on a lake in Alaska!

"Calm" can be an adjective, noun, or verb, depending on how it is applied. I recommend you apply it to your life in all forms. Here are some definitions from Dictionary.com:

Adjective: Not showing or feeling nervousness, anger, or other strong emotions.

Noun: The absence of violent or confrontational activity within a place or group.

Verb: To make (someone) tranquil and quiet; soothe. (Note: You can be that "someone"!)

LOOKING DEATH SQUARELY IN THE EYE

Back in the summer of 1984, when I was thirty-five, my family and I (along with many of the members of our executive team and board) traveled to Port Alsworth, Alaska (about 180 miles southwest of Anchorage), to stay at a fishing lodge for a week. Sixteen of us were seeking to get away from all the stresses of business and fish and unwind in Mother Nature. We had filled the lodge with our group, a combination of shareholders and directors of Pitcairn (a leading single family office).

This fishing lodge represented the quintessential Alaskan fishing experience. Two adults to a lakeside cabin, a huge hot tub, a sauna, horseshoes, volleyball, the main lodge with dining facilities, and a tackle shop. The living room area, complete with a hurricane woodstove and huge picture windows, overlooked an unbelievably picturesque bay, showcasing a jutting 5,000-foot Mt. Tanalian as its centerpiece. I guess you could describe it as "rustic decadence." With four fishermen to a plane, plus a pilot/guide, it all made for a truly unique and pampered

Alaskan wilderness experience. Even non-fishermen were blown away by seven days at this place.

Since I was already a licensed pilot and had previously been certified by the owner/operator of the lodge (a certified flight instructor), I was allowed to fly his Cessna 206 float planes used to fly to and from our fishing spots (ocean, lakes, and rivers only accessible by float planes). This afternoon, the pilot guide asked me to take the flight controls on our hour-long flight back to the lodge.

With confidence, I banked the Cessna 206 floatplane hard to the left, beginning a turn that would reveal that afternoon's first glimpse of the west end of Lake Clark. The lodge was only ten minutes away now. The warm Alaskan sun had produced a hothouse effect in our plane's cabin. I remember feeling a sense of pride as I piloted the plane, knowing I was the only one still awake. My passengers, including my father, brother, cousin, and pilot/guide, had all surrendered to sleep on the long ride home from a full day of king salmon fishing on the Mulchatna River.

More than an hour earlier, we had experienced a challenging takeoff, with no wind to aid our lift, a river run out shortened by a sandbar, and high trees. The floatplane stumbled into the air with a full load of passengers and an additional 200 pounds of salmon stuffed in both of the plane's pontoons. Following an initial climb out buffeted by thermals, the ride smoothed out and the engine droned monotonously. The eighty-four degrees in the cabin, coupled with a long day of fishing, complete with the traditional Alaskan shore lunch, provided my passengers with the ideal ingredients for a long siesta.

Ten miles down the lake, Mt. Tanalian's summit was a glistening beacon as the late afternoon sun reflected off its moist rocks. This familiar sight signaled that our landing in the cove opposite the lodge was only a few minutes away. Changing my grip on the yoke and scanning the instrument panel with particular attention to the altimeter, I eased the nose down to descend to 500 feet—my desired altitude in preparation for landing. The change in engine revs as I pushed the prop to full pitch, a steep bank to the right, and the grinding sound of twenty degrees of flaps woke my passengers.

I gently began to bring the plane's nose above the horizon. I tapped the throttle back in increments so my first contact with the water would be just inside the mouth of the cove. I didn't want any skips because I knew my passengers and the people lining the shore would scrutinize my technique.

Yes! I struck the landing. I knew I was lined up perfectly with the beach in front of the lodge. I cut the throttle, shut off the engine, and popped open the side window. Pete, the guide, also opened his door, and a delightful cool blast of air filled the cabin.

Normally, the end of my coast to the bank included a jerk and the sound of floats running onto the gravel. But with fish on board, the camp crew, fillet knives at the ready, caught the tip of the floats and spun us around so the tail could be pulled up on the bank and tied securely to the trees to the right of the lodge. The crew positioned us as close to the fish-cleaning table as our wing tip allowed. Before everyone and their gear were off the plane, our catch had been pulled from the hulls of the floats and was being cleaned. The beautiful pink meat of the king salmon was exposed with each pass of the knife.

As I jumped from the float into eighteen inches of water, I asked our guide, Pete, if he was still on for my Piper Super Cub lesson and sign off. He said sure, but he needed to check on the barbecue he was in charge of for the evening meal. I suggested we meet in forty-five minutes, and he agreed. This would give me ample time to get out of my fishing clothes, quickly jump in the hot tub, shower, and be ready for my turn in the Super Cub.

If everything went as planned, I would get Pete, the owner/operator of the lodge, to sign me off on his pride and joy—a new Super Cub (with an amped-up engine). Two years earlier, he had given me my check ride in one of his floatplanes. Now I could almost taste soloing in the Alaskan bush. Me in a Piper Super Cub—what a rush! One more ultimate flying experience and yet another bucket list goal checked off the list.

The bright yellow Piper Super Cub was parked just behind my cabin in a small clearing off to the side of the dirt road that led from the back of the main lodge to the rock-filled runway.

Arriving at the Super Cub first, I decided to get the pre-flight check out of the way. My thorough examination suggested everything was normal. I grabbed the prop and pulled the plane out of the clearing and onto the dirt road. When Pete showed up, he seemed pleased that I had everything ready to go. He climbed in the back and buckled in. I pulled myself up and into the front seat and fastened the shoulder straps in place with the seat belt. Pulling the manual fuel prime twice, I yelled out the window, "Clear!" Then I hit the starter and the engine caught.

Going light on the throttle during taxi reduced the risk of kicking a stick or rock into the prop and also caused less of a dust tornado to the surrounding cabins. As we bounced out to the side of the runway, I looked both ways for traffic. Seeing none, I pulled onto the runway and taxied down to the end nearest the bay. Brakes locked, run up and mag checks normal, flaps and trims set, fuel good, I asked Pete, "Are you ready?"

"Yes."

I swung the nose to the center line and began pushing up on the throttle smoothly. No need to hurry the acceleration; we had 4,800 feet of runway, long enough to land a DC-6 full of fuel and supplies. Pushing to full throttle, I hit forty-five miles per hour, pulled back on the stick, and we were airborne. At 200 feet, I dumped one notch of flaps, felt that sink, recovered the lost altitude, then dumped the second notch. Straight ahead, keep climbing, that was the ticket. After completing all the required safety, takeoffs, and landings for my flight check, I landed and let Pete out.

Oh, how I remember his words as he left: "Good luck, and remember it flies completely different with just one person on board." Neither of us could possibly have known how prophetic his words would be. Without Pete's weight, the Super Cub performed like a rocket ship. It had incredible power-to-weight characteristics.

The routine on the return from fishing was the same every day. A few minutes to compare fish stories as you unloaded the planes, then off to the hot tub, sauna, a nice cold shower, and, with glass in hand, a short stroll to the front deck of the main lodge for "cocktail hour."

I had planned for this day for more than a year. If I checked out in a Super Cub, I would surprise the cocktail crowd with an aerial display directly overhead. Having been granted my wings, it was show time! Since the element of surprise would certainly add to the theatrics of the aerobatics, I began by flying directly down lake, away from the lodge.

Eight miles later, I had gone far enough that my attack on Mt. Tanalian from the backside would go undetected by those on the deck. I dove through a small mountain pass. Long shadows from the late afternoon sun created vivid pictures along the way. The sound of the Super Cub startled a grazing moose in the mossy bog below. I was amazed by the incongruous grace of this huge animal as it took to the woods. It picked its steps carefully until its trot in the shallow water turned into a full gallop along the rocky beach before it darted into the deep underbrush. Beautiful shades of purple, green, blue, orange, yellow, brown, and white were among the colors of our Maker's palette that evening. A strange sense of peace and tranquility came over me as I marveled at God's beautiful creation.

Off in the distance, I spotted the back of Mt. Tanalian. Flying at a mere 200 feet above the valley floor, I would have a steep climb up the back spine to crest the 5,100-foot peak that could be seen from the lodge. I pushed up the throttle, pulled back on the stick, and imagined myself going up in an elevator and arriving at a penthouse. I experienced an amazing rate of climb at sixty-five miles per hour and felt a shudder as the plane accepted the challenge of my mountain assault.

With show time about to begin—in front of my father, guests, and coworkers—I could feel my heart begin to race. I anticipated the rush I would feel as my body reacted to the G-forces. The flight would be nothing crazy, mind you, but flashy to my audience. I planned a hammerhead stall with a kick over, then into a spin. That would be a good beginning, and then I would see what else felt right.

Just before reaching the summit, I saw a mountain goat and her baby perched on what appeared to be no more than a six-inch ledge suspended above an 800-foot crevice. All this nature, all this beauty, and the thrill of flying a Piper Super Cub in the Alaskan wilderness. I thought to myself, *Does it really get any better than this?*

The time had arrived for the games to begin. I had just enough clearance to buzz the peak...or did I? I had no more than ten feet of clearance as I skimmed the cliff on the front face of Mt. Tanalian. Then I was in the clear and could see everyone back at the lodge.

At 5,120 feet, I cleared the rocks. I pushed the nose over in a dive to build the required speed for my maneuvers. I increased my airspeed to seventy-five, eighty-five, 120 miles per hour, and finally 130 miles per hour, and when I reached 4,300 feet, I began to pull back on the stick. Then I thought, *Come on; don't be a wimp. Pull it hard into the seat pad.*

I continued to feel the G-forces pushing me hard into the bottom of the seat as I decelerated. That euphoric weightless feeling took over, and then my airspeed indicated a stall. It was time to add throttle, kick it over to the left with the rudder, and push forward on the stick.

Once I was at the peak of my arch, everything totally stopped. What a weird, yet peaceful, sensation. I was suspended in time and space.

My altimeter indicated 5,000 feet even. I kicked in the left rudder. The prop blast ensured the desired effect to the left. Now I pushed the throttle and simultaneously moved the stick forward.

The engine wound up—but wait a minute—the stick had not moved. It wouldn't move. It was jammed in my crotch! I felt the horrible feeling every pilot dreads—the stick was stuck and I had lost control of the plane. The reality of the stick locking up overcame me. I was out of control, and I found myself in an inverted flat spin.

I panicked!

The altimeter read 4,100 feet, but I was in free fall and an inverted flat spin. "I've got time," I told myself, but I had no parachute. I grabbed the flaps and had full movement there. I moved the throttle to idle. My stick was still stuck and had no movement, so I continued to both push and pull hard, but to no avail.

In that moment, with absolutely no control of the plane, I thought of Mara, my twelve-year-old daughter. I thought of her swimming in the championships back in Philadelphia this coming weekend. Her specialty was the backstroke, and she had a genuine shot at a league record. I saw her donning her cap and stepping up on her block, along with seven others also ready for the start. The starter raised their arm; the gun went off.

"Bang!" No, that was not a starter's gun—it was the flap's handle smashing down out of my hand onto its bracket. Next, I heard a voice say, "Dirk, you have to get your head back in this plane or you'll surely die." I felt like I was on drugs. It was as if I were in slow motion in a nightmare. Time separated in a big way. I didn't know whether I was reliving a prior experience, projecting myself into the future, or dealing with the present moment.

The sun blinded me during a spin, a chaotic somersault in the sky. It brought me back to the stark reality of my impending demise. It felt like only a moment ago I had cleared the peak and my flight was smooth, nothing to worry about. Again, I checked my altimeter. It read 2,850 and was falling fast. My airspeed was tough to read, being all over the place, but definitely in the red zone. I had too much speed and not enough altitude. I thought I was going to cannonball into the lake right in front of my father, my mentor, and my best friend! We would be celebrating my wife Judy's thirty-fifth birthday soon. I had planned on surprising her, but certainly not by crashing my plane into the lake in front of Dad.

Next, I heard, "Dirk, what the hell are you thinking about? For the last time, before you pack it in, try freeing the stick once more." I listened to the voice, braced my knees against the tubing on the sides of the fuselage for leverage, grabbed the stick, and pulled as hard as I could. I felt the stick begin to move.

No—it wasn't moving; it was bending.

Oh, God, I thought. *It's going to snap, but I've got to keep trying.* And I did.

I felt pressure against the back of the seat. *What's that?* I felt the seat being pushed forward. I thought, *It couldn't be pressure from the rear; that's strange.* I spun my head to look behind me. I was horrified when I saw why my stick was jammed, but I realized I at least had a chance. This Super Cub was the workhorse for remote construction projects at the camp and transported rafts and paddles to river locations. For maximum cargo capacity, the back of the rear seat had been removed and replaced with a backpack frame to allow long objects to be stuffed into the tail section.

The backpack frame, which was anchored at the bottom of the seat, had apparently gone weightless at the pinnacle of my previous maneuver, and in doing so, the top of the frame had come unfastened and fallen forward. The rear control stick was wedged between the heavy-duty nylon straps strung horizontally on its frame.

Knowing I had to free the rear stick to gain control, I grabbed the shoulder harness clasp to my seat belt, jerked it open, peeled back the straps around my back, and threw myself halfway into the backseat. But the vertigo I felt from so many spins made it almost impossible to function in the cramped space.

I grabbed the top of the frame with my right hand and realized I had to grab the front stick with my left hand and pull it back farther to release the pressure on the rear stick. All the while, I was perched atop the front seat. Somehow, I worked the backpack free of the rear stick.

I felt hope. I had a chance. I might not crash into the lake in front of God and everyone after all.

I struggled to get back into my seat and looked at the altimeter, which read 1,600 feet and falling. My airspeed was still too high. I had to get out of the inverted spin. With a full-functioning stick, I pushed it full forward to the left and applied full right rudder. I managed to stop the spin. Then, I eased the nose forward, and I was in a normal spin recovery.

I headed straight for the lake and thought, *I don't want to be too abrupt, or the wings might snap off.* I calculated the best dive recovery attitude with minimum clearance above the water. I pulled up and veered away from the lodge, and in doing so, showered the people on the deck with water from my trail. Having completely regained control, I flew out around the back of the camp into a downwind leg for my final approach to the runway. I landed smoothly after having cheated death moments earlier.

Wow, I had made it. I took several breaths and thanked God, the angels, the voices—whoever it had been who had kept me calm in this crisis so I could take quick, decisive action.

To this day, I don't remember much about the landing. I was totally numb. The first time I felt anything was back in the clearing behind the lodge where an hour earlier I had pre-flighted this bird.

I shut off the power, and with the Super Cub fully settled, I started to climb out of the cockpit. While climbing out, my right heel got caught under my seat and flipped me out onto the ground upside down. I lay there for a moment feeling the sweat pumping out of my body, hardly breathing, as the fall had knocked the breath out of me. I rolled over in the dust, pulled myself to my knees, and hugged the balloon tire to my chest, content just to hang on for a moment.

Then Pete came running down the lane and into the clearing. White as a ghost, knowing something terrible had happened, he said, "What the hell happened?" All I could do was point to the bent backpack frame in the rear seat. That was enough—he knew. With him there, I felt it was okay to relax—instead, I puked all over the tire I was hugging.

I was speechless. No words could capture my sheer terror and the emotions I felt after my near-death experience. With some time and distance, I recognized that, under extreme pressure, I had come through. This resilience and resourcefulness was something I could rely on during personal and professional challenges throughout life. But then Pete came over, helped me to my feet, and took me to my cabin.

With a shower and some clean clothes, I gathered my wits sufficiently to join the group for cocktails on the front deck. As I took a sip of a cold Coors, someone said, "Well, Dirk, that was a great first maneuver; why didn't you keep the show going?"

I was silent, figuring I could respond later, someplace else. I didn't feel the need to share the truth at that moment.

Near-death events are said to leave a lasting impression on those fortunate enough to live through them. To this day, the memories of that flight are indelibly etched into my mind. What I experienced was so vivid, so real, so scary, and yet so peaceful. The only way I can understand the peace that came over me is knowing that I was somehow able to remain calm in a nearly fatal crisis. Sometime later, I shared the truth with my father and Judy. They were so concerned, yet thankful my lucky stars had somehow guided me to safety that afternoon.

REMAINING CALM IN SERVICE TO OTHERS

Two-star General Ronald Nelson was one of my greatest mentors. I was blessed to have him as my high-school wrestling and football coach, physical education instructor, and geometry teacher.

General Nelson was a pilot who had flown President Eisenhower, the first president to use a helicopter for transportation. Nelson was one of the generals who shaped the training and boot camp course the Marines still use, known as "The Circuit Course." I was fortunate to have this circuit in my training program during my freshman year of wrestling. Like a drill sergeant, Nelson pushed us harder than we knew the human body could be pushed. His philosophy was if we were in better shape than our competition, we would have more confidence. His strategies apparently worked because we won nearly all our football games and most of our wrestling matches.

One afternoon in gym class, we were learning how to do back flips on the trampoline. General Nelson was spotting when one of his students got way too much air and came down near the edge of the trampoline. It was obvious his next jump would send him off the trampoline and crashing to the hard gym floor.

Nelson quickly and calmly moved into position to catch the student before he came crashing down onto the floor.

The student's heel struck the general's upper bicep, rupturing the bicep's tendon. Nelson calmly told us he needed "immediate medical attention," then drove himself to the hospital where the doctor reinserted the detached tendon.

This incident showed the value of remaining calm. Nelson's calm demeanor reminds me of what Roman Emperor Marcus Aurelius said: "The nearer a man comes to a calm mind, the closer he is to strength."

STAYING CALM UNDER FIRE

My son Jason became a paramedic when he was twenty-eight. He devoted his career to serving those in need by responding to their health emergencies. I had encouraged him to consider following in my footsteps in our family business, but after an internship in a similar operation, he decided it was not for him.

Rather, Jason discovered his love for physiology and the wonders of the human body. That happened after he worked with a career consultant who suggested he take the Myers-Briggs Personality Assessment course. Jason did so and found his calling. I couldn't be more proud of him for following his passions.

On his first day of work, Jason's team responded to a call at the home of a woman in a diabetic coma. Her daughter met Jason at the door. She was frantic and said her mother was downstairs, was a diabetic, and was not breathing.

Jason knew from his training that diabetics often have collapsed arteries and veins that make it almost impossible to administer life-saving medications. With this knowledge, he took quick action. He had a Dremel drill among his equipment and immediately drilled a large hole in the side of the patient's knee. Then he quickly screwed in a piece of plumbing to force fluids and medication directly into her bone marrow.

Jason and his partner got the patient on a gurney and into the ambulance. On the way to the hospital, they had to use cardiac paddles to revive her. Her daughter met them at the ER and expressed sincere and supreme gratitude for saving her mother's life. Again, this was all on Jason's first day as a paramedic.

Jason's quick thinking, fast action, and calm mindset reminds me of what James Allen, philosopher and author of *As a Man Thinketh*, said: "The more tranquil a man becomes, the greater is his success, his influence, his power for good. Calmness of mind is one of the most beautiful jewels of wisdom."

I believe remaining calm in a crisis can be your superpower if you focus on continuing to grow and evolve as a parent, spouse, entrepreneur, or community member. The goal is to keep improving and evolving so you can eliminate the stress of daily life and achieve everything humans crave: peace, love, joy, harmony, and prosperity. The current Dalai Lama, Tibet's great Buddhist teacher, spent a lifetime in prayer and meditation to achieve this way of life, which is why his thoughts on this subject are so powerful: "The greater level of calmness of our mind, the greater our peace of mind, the greater our ability to enjoy a happy and joyful life."

Another of my favorite quotes, which is from Lao Tzu, drives this point home: "To a mind that is still, the whole universe surrenders."

KEY POINTS FOR REMAINING CALM IN TIMES OF CRISIS

1. Determine If the Crisis Is a Matter of Life or Death: If it is clearly a matter of life or death, you must make immediate decisions and take swift action.

2. Take a Deep Breath: Often when you pause momentarily by taking a deep breath, you are, in essence, resetting your mind to pause, reflect, decide, and then take swift action.

3. Use Your Adrenaline to Achieve a Different State: Often, adrenaline kicks in during a crisis and may cause your thoughts to

be unclear. The key is to allow this adrenaline to put you in a different state to see the crisis more clearly and from a different angle and then assist you in taking the right action.

4. Take on a Single-Focused Action: Once you make the first decision, focus all of your efforts on executing that action while eliminating anything that can distract you.

5. Remove Yourself from the Situation: Pretend you are a third party looking in at the crisis, and then apply common sense from this perspective to clearly define the correct path forward.

6. Get Your Head Straight: When crisis hits, your mind might leave your body and reflect on other things such as how wonderful your life has been, your loved ones, and perhaps even the meaning of life. But at times like this, you need to put these important things out of your mind and focus on your next action.

7. Reflect After the Crisis: As was the case in Jason's career, young adults should try different careers early. Knowing what you don't find appealing is just as important as using career counseling to discover your strengths and interests.

8. Ask Yourself, "How Would My Father, Mother, Mentor, or Coach Respond to This Crisis?": I am sure you have people who shaped you into the person you are today. Perhaps it was a parent, partner, mentor, coach, or colleague. It could be anyone you respect for their morals, values, ethics, and character. Whoever the individual was (and you know who they are), ask yourself how they would respond, and then respond the same way to your crisis.

9. Most Importantly, Ask Yourself, "How Will This Crisis Effect My Family?": Since family is the most important thing in life, every decision you make in business, relationships, and taking

risk will affect your family somehow. Therefore, keep your family in mind when responding/reacting in a crisis.

EXERCISE

1. What crises have you survived? Which have made you a better, more skilled "pilot" in turbulent times? Describe what you learned about yourself in these experiences.

_____

_____

_____

_____

_____

_____

_____

_____

_____

2. Which quick reactions have not turned out well? What were the ramifications of reacting too quickly instead of responding with calmness and resolve?

_____

_____

_____

_____

_____

_____

_____

_____

_____

3. Which actions from the key points above are you committed to adding to decision making to help you remain calm in a crisis?

_____

_____

_____

_____

_____

_____

_____

Chapter 2
SEVEN RULES FOR MULTIGENERATIONAL FAMILY ENTERPRISES

"A hundred years from now,
it will not matter what my bank account was,
the sort of house that I lived in, or the kind of car I drove. But the world
may be better because I was important in the life of a child."

— Forest Witcraft

One definition of *family* (noun) is: groups of people who genuinely love, trust, care about, and look out for each other. A family can be a little bit crazy and a little bit loud, but they can have a whole lot of love.

Because I believe family is one of the most important things in the world, I have dedicated my life's work to preserving mine. The following are seven rules to live and work by if you, too, want to build a successful family enterprise. When you apply the following seven rules to your family enterprise, hopefully, you will experience great success.

My definition of a "family enterprise" includes: a family-operated business, a family office, family councils, family philanthropy, family trusts, family-sensitive real estate, and family archives/museum/art (heritage symbols).

RULE #1: WRITE RULES AND FOLLOW THEM

Create transparent, objective rules and follow them.

Recognizing the human condition requires a foundation of trust to sustain families, I have learned that "unwritten rules foster distrust," which is not what you want.

I am shocked by the number of families who are clear about governing their business and wealth but do not clearly share these rules with upcoming generations. In other words, the senior generation thinks the next generation is just going to get it...and often members of the upcoming generation inadvertently break the rules because they do not understand things like employment policies or proper communication channels and decision-making processes. Often education and/or professional experience are overlooked when looking at a family member's qualifications for a leadership position.

Governance 101 and Rules

All should be addressed by a family constitution—and include:

1. Bylaws

2. Documents of Incorporation

3. Fiduciary Responsibilities

4. Charters for Committees

5. Nominating Processes

6. Family Employment Policies

7. Liquidity Programs

Lessons of Rule #1

1. Create transparent, objective rules.

2. Follow them.

RULE #2: BEGIN WITH THE NEXT GENERATION IN MIND

Everything you do in a family business enterprise should be based on doing what is right today *and* for future generations. *Succession planning* is a process, not an event. In other words, it takes time and must be repeated and repeated and repeated. Once you complete a transition plan for leadership, get ready to do the next one.

Generational transition is risky business! Some ways of focusing on the next generation are to include and invite them to participate in many of the activities below. This is how to build a family's connective tissue.

- Family Newsletter (digital works)

- Family Archives (archival digs are fun)

- Programs Honoring Family Elders (Indigenous American cultures do a great job of respecting their elders)

- Family Talent Shows (This is how you get maximum attendance at family meetings)

- Family Website

- Affinity Trips (scuba diving trips, safaris, etc.)

- Internships/Experiences

- Philanthropy (Treat this as an investment)

- Family Banks

- Family Values and Behavior Exercises

Lessons of Rule #2:

1. Because of modern technology, many of these activities can be performed remotely.

2. Find family members to champion these causes.

3. This is a great opportunity to foster leadership development for the next generation.

RULE #3: BE TRUE TO FAMILY VALUES AND SPREAD THE STORY

This is a great opportunity to regularly review and reaffirm and/or change the foundational values of the family business enterprise. I suggest repeating elements of the values exercise outlined below every five years.

Dennis Jaffe's Family Value Vetting Process

A trained facilitator has a deck of fifty-two cards. A family/enterprise value is written on each. Ask family/enterprise members to sort the cards into piles with their first choice on top and moving down through their seventh choice. The other cards may be important, but they aren't among their primary values. Then the group is encouraged to share their seven priorities with the others. The next step in the process is to share each value along with a story about how and when they first realized that value was important to them. Stories connect people. Depending on the size of the group, the goal is to move from individual values to shared values. Through this process, the family ends up with their seven most important values. Then they use the cards to build a pyramid with a base of four cards, the next level has three, and there are two at the top—the most important values. This is called the *Family Value Pyramid*. Thanks to Dennis Jaffe and Caroline Bailey, whose "FEAT" (family enterprise assessment tool) values assessment tool is becoming the Kleenex of family value exercises.

This process will never disappoint. Some may be reluctant to share at first, but they are likely to become the experience's biggest fans.

Lessons of Rule #3:

1. Family value work is one of the key responsibilities and deliverables of a "Family Council." I will go into this important family vehicle more deeply later.

2. Spend time and money on this aspect of your family's enterprise. You will not be disappointed.

3. Ensure all participants get to speak and share their stories.

4. This is an initial pass at determining the foundational values of the family enterprise—consider using a consultant; possibly develop a family member to lead this activity in the future.

5. Once you have distilled your family's core values, identify habits and rituals that will amplify these values in your family's actions.

RULE #4: SEE THE BIGGER WEALTH PICTURE

Ensure all forms or capital are respected in the family's work.

I want to give credit to my good friend Jay Hughes for his work on the many forms of capital that help family enterprises. Each form of capital has a unique place in a family system. (See below for five types of capital.)

Not everyone in the family has the same appreciation, understanding, and respect for the family wealth. (Some may take it for granted or focus only on the financial capital and not realize capital is also social, spiritual, human, and intellectual.)

This is where you include five forms of capital, five areas for a bigger picture:

1. Spiritual Capital—because individuals discern their unique gifts, strengths, and charity there.

2. Financial Capital—the quantitative aspects of assets.

3. Social Capital—identify the core practice of the family.

4. Human Capital—is every member of the family flourishing?

5. Intellectual Capital—what do you know? Are you a continuous learning system?

Lesson of Rule #4:

Take time within the family enterprise to *fairly value* shared assets; this is essential. Early education about majority and minority stakeholders' interests in the enterprise and the related lessor valuation or discounts for a minority stake is important for building trust in developing and explaining approaches to valuation. Often, minority stakeholders receive 25-30 percent less than majority stakeholders.

RULE #5: PRUNE WHEN NECESSARY

Each generation may need to do some pruning. This may come from the organization's need for change or from an individual who wants out.

In pruning, the organization must be willing to let go of certain branches (individuals) should they choose to free themselves from the central family enterprise. This means some offspring may not want to be part of the family enterprise. They are certainly welcome to pursue their own career path and values, but this may mean they no longer benefit from the family enterprise.

If some want to take their family marbles and go somewhere else, they are welcome to do so. Because if you take away freedom of choice, you put dynamite on the tracks, and it becomes only a matter of time before someone ignites the dynamite, putting the whole family and its enterprise at risk.

Lessons of Rule #5:

1. To prevent a risk exposure, implement a fair and objective system to help members exit the enterprise when necessary/attractive.

2. Enterprise governance structures need the authority to prune when necessary.

RULE #6: DEVELOP EFFECTIVE COMMUNICATION SYSTEMS

An example of what not to do arose when I was head of Client Services for Pitcairn. One key complaint from a client survey was our communication structure was ineffective. I should have formed a focus group to help develop a new reporting package to deal with the complaints. Instead, I went to my competitors to look at their packages. I came back with what I thought was a complete and wonderful reporting package. It was as thick as a phone book, yet totally missed the mark. If I had asked my clients for their views on what a new reporting package should look like, it would have been far better.

The moral to the story is communication is often more about asking and listening than talking—the former being much more likely to get buy-in. As a service provider, you are given two ears and one mouth for a reason. Remember "silent" and "listen" use the same letters, just in a different order.

The bottom line is the majority of threats to family enterprises come from poor communication, so when you communicate effectively, you prevent most issues.

Four Keys to Effective Communication:

1. Communicate openly and often.

2. Be transparent.

3. Be timely.

4. Be relevant.

Lessons of Rule #6

1. An organization's effectiveness is directly related to how it communicates.

2. Leaders need to be accountable for their communications.

3. Your target audience needs to be included in designing communications.

4. The four keys listed above are the primary concerns.

RULE #7: PROMOTE ENTREPRENEURSHIP IN THE PERSONAL AND PROFESSIONAL LIVES OF THE FAMILY

The ongoing connectedness of the family is ensured when storytelling is a priority. This is important because entrepreneurship is one of the only known antidotes to the shirtsleeves to shirtsleeves in three generations phenomenon among family groups.

This will be where the 4Rs come into play. Each generation needs to be encouraged to strive for the 4Rs in developing a process committed to each new generation.

- Re-Imagine (the future)

- Re-Invent (the purpose)

- Re-Invest (commit to a capital plan)

- Re-Passion (this is a Dirk-ism)

Later, I will dedicate all of Chapter 11 to the idea behind the 4Rs.

Usually, about the time a family needs to be entrepreneurial and take a risk, they go into scarcity mode instead. Taking calculated risks as part of re-generation and renewal is essential to establishing and achieving family goals. When we think we only have a certain amount of money, we tend to hoard it. Maybe families haven't learned how to earn money, so they are afraid to lose it.

Most wealth management firms' service offerings sound the same, but Pitcairn's comprehensive wealth advisory services focus on creating wealth momentum.

Lessons of Rule #7

1. Don't be afraid to take calculated risks.

2. If you learn how to earn money, you won't be afraid of losing it.

FAMILY ENGAGEMENT

I have spent my life looking for ways to continuously engage and involve multiple family generations. Whether it is a family business or shared wealth and philanthropy, regular family meetings are essential for sustaining the family.

And remember, even with today's digital meeting options, don't forget to also provide personal gatherings.

FAMILY SYSTEM/FAMILY COUNCILS

A family council's effectiveness is directly proportional to their ability to engage the entire family. The key deliverables for family councils is facilitating ongoing, relevant family meetings and ongoing training and education. One way of maintaining participation is identifying activities family members enjoy. Without this, it is difficult to keep families interested in attending family meetings.

In the Pitcairn's case, our family council developed a networking tool we called "Relativity." This secure database of family addresses, interests, and careers included a function for letting the broader family communicate if they were open to other family members dropping by for a visit. You flew a green flag for yes and a red for no.

The goal of family meetings is twofold: to update the family on its business and wealth and promote sustainable family connectedness.

GETTING FAMILY TO SHOW UP FOR MEETINGS (THE GLUE THAT BINDS)

1. Identify family members with the skills and interests to take on an archival dig of family history and legacy. Websites such as Ancestry.com help families understand and maintain family histories. Digital newsletters capture family members' activities in their personal and professional lives, like births, memorials, awards, graduations, careers/jobs, and hobbies/interests, which come together to form an active network.

2. A popular activity ensuring high participation is the family night talent show. It fosters group involvement in family meetings. I suggest the family council chair's most important job is organizing family meetings. Larger family meetings seem to work best when held every two years.

3. Find family songs. The goal is to find a song the entire family knows and likes, and essentially, this song becomes the family theme song. Over the years, as more people marry into the family, be open to new songs to bless the family with to foster an environment of inclusion. Below are two examples of our family theme songs:

Pitcairn's Family Song: "Crambamboli"

First Verse: *Crambamboli, Crambamboli, here's to the whole grand family. The whole grand family Crambamboli.*

Second Verse: *Crambamboli, Crambamboli, here's to the whole grand family. Cram bim bam bamboli, Crambamboli.*

Pitcairn's Family Song: "I Found a Horseshoe"

I found a horseshoe, I found a horseshoe. I picked it up and hung it o'er the door.

It was all rusty and full of nail holes. Good luck, good luck, good luck forever more.

I found a horseshoe, I found a horseshoe, I picked it up and hung it o'er the door.

It was all rusty and full of nail holes. Good luck, good luck forever more.

4. Family internships help get young family members involved. For either the business or family wealth, it is important for young family members to work in and learn the family business and or about its wealth, and focus on the family communication that goes with keeping both the family and the family business together.

5. Put together family "plays" that honor senior generations and the family legacy and that are played out by current generations. Doing so not only shows respect, but also adds lots of humor in a unique historical perspective. These types of activities bring the family closer together.

6. Also, create "Family Olympics" to foster a healthy and competitive environment, but avoid allowing such events to get too competitive.

7. Tell family stories. This might be the most important way to attract people and maintain connectivity across generations. Also, these stories not only teach family history and reinforce family values, but they add warmth, humor, and connectedness to meetings.

METHODS OF DEALING WITH FAMILY DISCORD (THE FRICTION THAT FRACTURES)

The three major ways of dealing with family discord are:

1. Liquidity programs. Lack of liquidity, as I mentioned, equals dynamite on the tracks. Therefore, governance has a responsibility to provide ongoing liquidity to members with clear and fair valuation by an independent party.

2. Reducing potential for family discord often comes down to a family commitment to *inclusion* over *exclusion*. Failure to include in-laws in the family dynamic can quickly produce outlaws. An often seen family enterprise failure is being unclear about the roles of the various constituents. Leaders must know the family rules dealing with governance structure, family employment policies, and qualifications for trusteeships, directorships, and being a constructive owner. Note that it is detrimental to a family business when members working within the enterprise have more perks than those who don't. The point is to ensure an independent member of the board chairs the enterprise's compensation programs. Without that, jealousy can eat at the trust needed to sustain the future family business enterprise.

3. Family councils are responsible for identifying family conflicts and recommending ways of resolving them.

DIRKISMS

Here are some of my favorite quotes about sustaining family enterprises. (I call them Dirk-isms):

1. Your choice: programs that foster connectedness or be subject to dissolution.

   "The glue that binds or the friction that fractures."

2. This quote is one that a fellow family business consultant and I developed after seeing Swiss road signs. Again, your choice:

   "When you go fast, you go alone. If you want to go far, go together."

3. And finally, Simon Sinek said:

   "If we were good at everything, we'd have no need for each other."

I believe Sinek means we need family to take the best wisdom, experience, talent, and knowledge and apply it to the whole family, and as a result, the whole family benefits! Understand that positive results require care and time.

KEY POINTS OF SEVEN RULES FOR MULTIGENERATIONAL FAMILY ENTERPRISES

1. Create and understand bylaws that benefit the family for generations.

2. Create documents of incorporation.

3. Clearly define fiduciary responsibilities.

4. Create clear and logical charters for committees.

5. Develop a fair, clear, and sustainable nominating processes for family enterprise governance.

6. Establish clear family employment policies.

7. Ensure liquidity programs are in place that allow members to exit if they choose.

EXERCISE

1. Which of the above seven rules resonates most with you? How so?

_____

_____

_____

_____

_____

_____

_____

2. What does family engagement mean to you? Which of the above strategies will you incorporate to help achieve family engagement?

_____

_____

_____

_____

_____

_____

_____

3. Which of the above three strategies are you going to incorporate into your family business to prevent friction and fractures?

_____

_____

_____

_____

_____

_____

Successful Families Build Thoughtfully Together:

Go Far, Go Together.

Go Fast, Go Alone.

Chapter 3

LEVERAGING THE POWER OF PUBLIC/PRIVATE PARTNERSHIPS

"When public and private sectors combine intellectual and other resources, more can be achieved."

— Gro Harlem Brundtland

THE DEVELOPMENT OF THE NATIONAL DIGITAL LIBRARY

Back in the early 1990s, when I was in my forties, a good friend, Gerry Lenfest of the James Madison Council of the Library of Congress (LOC), encouraged me to join him and John Kluge, founder of Metro Media and a cable mogul, to help bring in the private sector to digitize the vast Library of Congress collection (located in the Jefferson Building in Washington, DC).

Before this effort, only researchers had access to the LOC collection. And even with a $500 million annual budget, not one dollar was allocated for this project. Dating back to 1800, the Library of Congress is the nation's oldest federal cultural institution. It is housed in the Jefferson Building because Thomas Jefferson donated his library to this collection. The LOC is the largest library on the planet, with more than 140 million items, including maps, newspapers, newsreels, movies, books, songs, records, inventions, and poems, and it is always growing. Every patent that has ever been granted is also located here.

The James Madison Council was made up of a hundred individual businesspeople, philanthropists, and celebrities. I felt honored to be the youngest member of the council. Through my membership, I had the pleasure of meeting and developing a close working relationship with James Earl Jones. He is the voice of Darth Vader in *Star Wars* among many other movie roles. I also met Betsy Bloomingdale, Ross Perot, Jerry Jones, Ed Cox, and got reacquainted with FedEx founder Fred Smith.

Speaking of FedEx, I also met Francis McGuire. He was the marketing consultant who developed the KFC advertising campaign featuring Colonel Sanders. He also developed a number of ads for FedEx. He thought he had a great idea to rebrand FedEx as the nation's best airline, which was a complete failure. However, he went on to find the phrase, "When it absolutely, positively has to be there overnight."

McGuire brought this concept back to FedEx, and of course, it was a huge success. With the success of the campaign, McGuire set up a trust fund for the FedEx employees' three children for their college tuition. McGuire also taught me the phrase, "Opportunity is nowhere," which spelled differently reads: "Opportunity is now here." This is a helpful perspective when dealing with conflict.

Additionally, I want to recognize the important leadership of Dr. James Billington, the head librarian, and his wife Marjorie Billington, who were the ultimate gracious hosts for many of the James Madison Council meetings and events.

The Library of Congress James Madison Council raised $200 million in three years, which led to six million pieces of history being digitized. The council helped launch the nation's digital library and develop an extensive curriculum for use in educational systems around the globe. These early efforts led to virtually all of today's libraries having access to this new digitization approach to library science and its advantages.

I believe I was personally responsible for cancelling more than fifteen brick-and-mortar building projects around the country to hold hard copy materials once we recognized the power of the digital age LOC.

To raise awareness of this new educational resource, we went to each of the 435 congressional districts and asked each to be part of the new digital library by identifying something indigenous to their district that could be captured in digital form and be part of the LOC's two-hundredth anniversary. Two districts from my home state of Pennsylvania made bicentennial quilts. And from Chadds Ford, Pennsylvania, a member of the Wyatt family painted a landscape capturing the beauty of their countryside.

I was also part of a group selected to approach First Lady Hillary Clinton to ask that the White House display these gifts. Clinton was warm, cordial, and accommodating.

To encourage attendance at the semi-annual meeting of the James Madison Council, members were assigned a librarian to make the vast collection available to. As part of this process, I had the pleasure of holding George and Martha Washington's love letters in my hands. I also got to hold the diary of Wilbur and Orville Wright in which they wrote about the run up to their first flight at Kitty Hawk. Both were significant experiences I will forever treasure.

The rollout of the national digital library and its programs as part of the library's two-hundredth birthday was a resounding success in 2000. I am very humbled to have worked with such a great group of people on an incredibly important technological achievement for our country and the globe.

FORMATION OF AN IMPORTANT LAND CONSERVATION

My mother's first cousin was Feodore (Feo) Pitcairn, who was an executive and trustee with the Pitcairn Company and was Chair of Pitcairn between my father and me. As a dedicated environmentalist and philanthropist, he saw the importance of land conservation in Eastern Montgomery County, Pennsylvania. We live in a part of the county with rolling hills, important water supplies, beautiful fields, and old-growth forests. The Burroughs of Bryn Athyn had seen much development in the neighboring townships. Feo had seen firsthand the pristine Pennypack Creek go from an area where neighbors could swim, picnic, and fish, to a polluted stream that had become a dumping ground for tires, mattresses, and old refrigerators. As a result, volunteers came together to clean up the creek, and after the initial success, Feo and others saw the benefit of forming a charitable trust to ensure the creek's water quality and reserve land as permanent open space for the generations to come. Feo asked me to join the Pennypack Trust board as treasurer, and of course, I accepted.

Coming back to the idea of public/private partnerships, the Pitcairn family and their trusts owned substantial acreage in the center of the Pennypack Ecological Restoration Trust (PERT). Pitcairn family members decided to transfer ownership to the trust at a bargain price. We got the highest and best appraisal to ascertain the value we used to calculate the Pitcairn Trusts tax deduction, which allowed us to transfer the property to PERT at a much lower value. We incorporated public monies from open space funding in three adjoining townships, and the business community, including banks, got involved. We went to private foundations to get their support and reached out to individuals to contribute. Coordinating contributions from many people became an integral part of preserving the Pennypack open space for future generations.

The 200-acre property we contributed was known as Raytharn Farms. Raytharn Farms was named for my great-grandfather's three sons, Raymond, Theo, and Harold. Today, more than 750 acres are preserved as open space in perpetuity. Also, Rutgers and Penn State have researched the unique benefits of this open space among the development of the Delaware Valley in the Philadelphia suburbs. Over the years, neighbors have committed another 500 acres of open space, making this area 1,250 acres. This project is a perfect example of the good that can come from public and private cooperation in making the world a better place.

KEY POINTS FOR LEVERAGING THE POWER OF PUBLIC/ PRIVATE PARTNERSHIPS

1. Harness collaborative effort to achieve great results that benefit the public but may not be achieved solely by government or private entities alone.

2. Enhance education opportunities through technological advancements. The Library of Congress is a go-to website.

3. Recognize and leverage the power of networking.

4. Commit to preserving open space that protects the environment for future generations.

5. One of the greatest benefits of being a family member of a successful family enterprise is the good that can come from being able to give back and make the world a better place. I feel fortunate to have grown up in a family that has always been committed to philanthropic causes.

EXERCISE

1. What public/private partnerships do you admire in your community?

_____

_____

_____

_____

_____

_____

2. What connections do you have in either the public or private sector that could help facilitate win-win opportunities for your family business?

_____

_____

_____

_____

_____

_____

3. Identify two or three potential joint venture opportunities you could facilitate to benefit both your family business and local community.

_____

_____

_____

_____

_____

Chapter 4
TEACHING FOUNDATIONAL FAMILY VALUES

"The family has always been the cornerstone of American society.
Our families nurture, preserve, and pass on to each
succeeding generation the values we share and cherish,
values that are the foundation of all our freedoms."

— Ronald Reagan

My mother and father made it a point to include all their children and their growing families in weeklong summer vacations. As my children grew up and started leading their own lives, I included them in family vacations. One particular year included three generations of the Jungé family, including my siblings and our children—one big clan heading to Prince Edward Island, Canada.

The resort had cabins. My four adult children ranging in age from twenty-three to twenty-six—one having recently married and the others with their significant others—all came on this trip. Our kids said, "Dad, you always tell us about all the great things you do for other families, so why don't you show us a little love on this trip and treat us to some of your good work?"

I picked one of my go-to exercises, helping family groups form their family values statements. About a week before we met, I sent an invitation letter to them and my wife Judy, saying in part:

No, I didn't just read another book or hear an inspirational speaker on this topic of family values. I have learned that setting and living by common values has proved to be the foundation for high-performing families. I wanted our family also to establish our own family values that will help us maintain constructive family dynamics. So here we go. This vacation can be a kick-starter of values to get all of you thinking along the lines of what is important to you, but please don't be limited by that. Please identify seven values that speak to you. See you soon. Love, Dad/Dirk.

To determine their values, they each needed to take a self-inventory and rank the tendencies on the continuum below. I asked them to place an X on the line to help them see where they stand on each of these character traits with O being the midpoint:

Cautious _____ O_____ Impulsive

Thrifty _____ O_____ Extravagant

Organize _____ O_____ Disorganized

Suspicious _____ O_____ Trusting

Impatient _____ O_____ Patient

Indirect _____ O_____ Direct

Indecisive _____ O_____ Decisive

Focused _____ O_____ Unfocused

Pessimistic _____ O_____ Optimistic

Inner-Directed _____ O_____ Outer-Directed

Lazy _____ O_____ Diligent

Defeatist _____ O_____ Resilient

Since Judy and I had the largest cabin, it seemed like the best location to hold our afternoon family meetings. In preparation, I secured a flip chart and several markers. I began this important family session with a prayer and then described the process we would use, which I had performed with many other families. The process included each of us describing an important family value, when we first experienced the value, and the story behind its importance.

When I finished setting the stage, my eldest daughter came up, put her arm around my shoulder, took my Sharpie, and said her penmanship was better than mine, so I should go sit down. This is true, but what she really wanted was for her dad to be fully present and part of the session. She wanted me to be part of the group and recognized my role needed to change. She's a teacher.

We spent three hours identifying our foundational family values and listening to stories about why they were important. The session lasted so long that we ended up being late for dinner with the rest of the clan.

Below is an example of many of our family values, some of which we added to our whiteboard:

Being Self-Motivated	Being Independent
Pursuing Excellence	Having Authority Over Others
Challenging Myself Intellectually	Having Job Security
Feeling Needed and Appreciated	Being Creative
Influencing Others	Taking Risks
Having Status	Being Well-Liked
Gaining New Knowledge	Working for the Environment
Preserving Wealth	Having Major Accomplishments
Being Active in the Community	Having Time Freedom

Making My Own Decisions	Being Content with My Work
Challenging Myself Athletically	Spending Time with Family
Having High Income	Being Spiritually Strong
Being Loyal at Work	Having Low Work Stress
Being Competitive	Being a Good Parent
Having Interests Outside of Work	Being an Ethical Person
Advancing My Career	Open-Mindedness
Being Well-Known	Fairness
Having Integrity	Humor
Having Power	Kindness
Serving Others	

Having heard each value, we went through the process of reducing our list of nearly forty to our seven core values. The process was important and very emotional. We all saw competition had played a significant role in our personal and professional development. Although we all saw the benefits of competition, two of my children had experienced the downside of competition within our own family when they were locked in arguments where one had to be right, making the other wrong instead of acknowledging they saw the same information from different perspectives, which left the impression of differing opinions. This revealed the dark side of competition between two of them, and it was affecting the whole family. They took full advantage of our session being a safe environment to discuss their differences. They each came up with a plan for respecting the other, allowing them to deescalate potential arguments, and they agreed in the future, when this tension arose, they needed to say "please respect" as the signal to change gears.

This understanding allowed them to see a given situation differently and still love and respect each other, despite their differences in experience and beliefs.

Had it not been for the family value session where this emotional issue could be aired, they might not have a good relationship today. Both realized unconditional love for each other, despite their differences, allowed them to strengthen their relationship and reduce family anxiety about their relationship. We all left that afternoon with a new sense of family connectedness.

This family meeting was in late July. Afterward, I took the values we identified to a friend who was a watercolor artist. The artist did a painting of an oak tree where the core values were the roots, but every value was depicted in the branches. At Christmas, I gave each of my children a copy of this tree displaying our foundational family values. All of my children proudly display this art in their homes, and they have said it is one of the best Christmas presents ever, which was very emotional and powerful for me.

LOVING UNCONDITIONALLY FROM DIFFERENT PERSPECTIVES

I suspect we are not the only family who has members who see issues, problems, challenges, beliefs, or philosophies differently. Does this sound familiar to you? Is it an issue in your family?

If so, where/how is it playing out in your business or within your family? See what you can do to bring in the differing parties to talk things out. Explain the "6/9 debate" and create a safe container for emotionally charged issues.

The 6/9 debate is where, from one perspective, one person clearly sees a 6, while the other person, perhaps because they are standing on the other side of the number, clearly sees a 9.

When both parties realize each is correct and their belief is only different because they see the situation from a different perspective, it can change the way they approach the future because they will quickly see how their 6 turns into a 9 and how their counterpart's 9 quickly turns into a 6.

The lesson is that everyone is different. Everyone's experiences, past, upbringing, gender, education, etc. dictates their point of view. When you teach others to understand and accept these differences and choose to love the other unconditionally, conflicts can be resolved or avoided altogether. As the parent or the owner of your business, I encourage you to teach this understanding and know that perspectives are different, but we can still choose to love, accept, and respect others. When you can do that, conflict can be avoided, and peace can be realized.

LEVERAGE YOUR CULTURE

Recently, as part of a monthly commitment to my Vistage leadership group, I was thrilled to meet our guest resource, David Friedman, whose topic was "How to Leverage Your Culture as a Strategic Advantage."

He reminded us of the expression "Culture eats strategy for breakfast." This expression has helped me understand behaviors are more effective in establishing culture in a family and its enterprise than values and why and how to make this a new paradigm shift. Thanks, David! For more about David, visit his website: www.CultureWise.com.

I actually think a combination of values exercises and David's approach to ritualizing behaviors will cement your culture and "make culture come alive."

KEY POINTS FOR TEACHING FOUNDATIONAL FAMILY VALUES

1. Try to bring family together at least once a year.

2. Establish and record family values as a group.

3. Teach the 6/9 debate to ensure family understands most of their differences come from seeing from a different perspective.

EXERCISE

1. Which family values have been passed down to you from your parents and grandparents' generations?

_____

_____

_____

_____

2. Which family values have you discovered are important to you that you also want to pass down to your children and grandchildren?

_____

_____

_____

_____

3. Which of the chapter's listed values resonate with you and will now be incorporated into your family business enterprise?

_____

_____

_____

_____

_____

Chapter 5

LEARNING FROM YOUR ANCESTORS AND MENTORS

"May strong roots hold you...while you reach for the sky."

— Hannah Dorman

Today in Pittsburgh, Pennsylvania, a sign created in 1983 by the Pennsylvania Historical and Museum Commission that commemorates the founding of Pittsburgh Plate Glass Company (PPG) resides on Fourth Avenue. PPG was co-founded by John Pitcairn, Jr., my great-grandfather. During his long and industrious career, he blessed so many employees, customers, and family members throughout the world. (The spacing as shown below is exactly as it reads on the sign.)

PITTSBURGH PLATE GLASS COMPANY

First commercially successful U.S. plate glass maker, founded 1883 by John Ford, John Pitcairn and others. First plant was at Creighton; office was a half block east of here on Fourth Avenue. The company became PPG Industries in 1968.

Let me take you back to the beginning and show you how all this came about.

FAMILY HERITAGE AND LEGACY

Many people over the years have struggled with the pronunciation of my last name Jungé. I am proud of my last name because it was given to me by my father, James, and he was entrusted with it by his father, William, and of course, William got it from his forefathers.

The Jungé family hails from Barr, a small town on the Rhine River in Alsace-Lorraine (now called Alsace-Moselle), an area in France near the border with Germany. Sometimes it has been part of France and sometimes part of Germany, depending on the winds of war.

Around 1800, Napoleon dragged his battered troops into Barr where one of my relatives was the mayor. Napoleon begged for sustenance for his troops. As the story goes, my ancestor put on a celebration and feast featuring wine, women, and song. At the end of the three days of "R and R," as Napoleon gathered his troops to return to Paris, he said to my ancestor, "You have done such a kindness for France! Unfortunately, I have no funds for repaying your kindness. I will, therefore, give you a sign of French nobility, the accent 'aigu' as my pledge to return and make full payment." I believe, as the story concludes, Napoleon stiffed us because he never returned, but we retained the accent "aigu" in our last name Jungé.

Our family's Scottish heritage comes from my mother's side. One relative was John Pitcairn, a major with the Scottish troops in the Revolutionary War who fired the "shot heard round the world," which started the American Revolution. Many people don't realize the Scots, as part of Great Britain, were among those fighting against the Continental Army. Major Pitcairn died two months later at the battle of Bunker Hill.

I have always said the Pitcairns are passionate, but not always on the right side of conflict. Today, our family proudly displays a replica of Major Pitcairn's pistol in the Pitcairn offices.

Pitcairn Island is a remote island in the South Pacific. John Pitcairn's son Robert was a midshipman on Her Majesty's Ship *The Swallow* in the South Pacific. It was the custom at the time for whoever spotted an unnamed landmass to name it, usually after themselves. Robert Pitcairn was in the crow's nest when he spotted the unnamed island. Pitcairn Island became famous when the *Bounty* mutineers with their leader Fletcher Christian arrived in their long boats.

JAMES FRANCIS JUNGÉ

My father, James Francis (called Jim by everyone), was born on June 18, 1921. He turned out to be an awesome husband, father, grandfather, and role model for many. He came from a meager background since he lost his own father (William) at eight. He had poor eyesight, which kept him out of the military, so he could not serve in World War II. During the war, he put himself through the chemical engineering program at the University of Illinois, earning his degree in two-and-a-half years. He paid for his tuition, food, and supplies by washing dishes for three different fraternities.

After graduation, he married my mother, and they had seven children. I was third. Dad's first job was as a research scientist for Gulf Oil in Pittsburgh. There he developed the catalytic process for removing sulfur from crude oil. This invention allowed military aircraft to fly higher and longer missions without carboning (carbon buildup reducing the power and efficiency of the engines). He felt this was his contribution to the war effort and our pilots. I asked if he was paid for the patent on this process. He said he got twenty-five dollars and was happy because he was being paid to do research.

Dad spent his life demonstrating the benefits of hard work. He was a strong proponent of collaboration and partnering to achieve organizational goals. When I married Judy, my high school sweetheart, on June 18, 1971, Dad's fiftieth birthday, he said a new daughter-in-law was one of the best birthday gifts ever. He absolutely loved Judy.

The community in which I was raised is a Swedenborgian Christian faith-based community where the church followed the Episcopal form of governance. The bishop was seen as the CEO of the educational system and the ministry. While our bishops were very good at pastoring, they were not always so good at strategic planning, raising capital, or running schools. To address these issues, Dad formed a meaningful partnership between the priest and the laity. This meant businesspeople could oversee the endowments, be involved in fundraising, and handle the mission of overseeing the church and its subsidiaries. My father was a key figure in supporting the church and school systems throughout the globe for this small Christian Church.

FLIGHT

My father went out of his way to support me unconditionally in all my endeavors. One example of his support came in 1986 when he took Judy and me to Maui to celebrate our fifteenth anniversary. The trip featured my first helicopter flight in a Papillon helicopter. On the flight, with the headsets blaring the theme from *2001: A Space Odyssey*, we flew into a canyon to the bottom of the 2,000 foot waterfall and slowly ascended up to the top of the waterfall, stopping halfway up to look at a parrot clinging to the wall of the cliff. After the accent, we flew to the top of the Hale'akala crater. We dove down into the heart of the crater; then as we were flying out, we flew beside a thunderstorm and were treated to a 180-degree rainbow. Then we flew out over the channel between Maui and Molokai and hovered twenty feet over a mother humpback whale and her calf, witnessing multiple spouts from their blow holes. Although I was a fixed-wing pilot already, I had never experienced anything so captivating. I knew in that moment I had to become a helicopter pilot.

When we got home, I couldn't stop thinking I was meant to be a helicopter pilot. I remember many dreams of flying, and I was totally consumed with making it happen! I had often been told I was a natural pilot. That did not prove to be the case when I tried to master helicopter flight. My initial lessons were made up of moving the helicopter from one landing circle to the next on a large, concrete pad with six landing circles. I was encouraged to move from one circle to another in a hover, which is the most difficult aspect of flying a helicopter. I thought I might end up killing myself and my instructor with my ineptness. This was in contrast to my beautiful intentions and plans of being as skilled a helicopter pilot as the pilot in Maui. Of course, I didn't have the thousands of hours of piloting that the Maui pilot had, but I was disappointed with my inability to fly this bird safely. Nonetheless, I was determined and prevailed.

Remember the exhilaration of mastering a two-wheeled bike? Mastering a helicopter was about ten times that. So, after learning on a Hughes 300 piston driven helicopter (the old whirly bird), I wanted to progress to turbine executive cabin helicopters for greater range and passenger capacity. And that is where my dad came in. I needed him to partner with me on the purchase of an A-star Aerospatiale helicopter for my personal and charter business use.

Since the expenses of such an endeavor were high, I decided to form a 135 charter operation so other people could help me pay for my habit. Initially, Dad was somewhat reluctant to join in my venture. But my first instructor was a skilled professional helicopter pilot, and I chose him to be the lead pilot in my new venture. I talked my dad into converting a perfectly good dairy barn on his property into a heliport and hanger for Helicopter Services, Inc. (which became the legal name of our entity).

After ten years of failing to make money with the helicopter operation, at the year-end meeting, my dad, who was an equal partner and had to pay his share of the constant reinvestment of funding for operations, said: "Dirk, why do you keep calling this a business? When things I like to do cost money, I call those hobbies!" He also said I had taken over key leadership positions in the Pitcairn Company that amounted to more than a full-time job.

Dad suggested we change our lead pilot's compensation and job title, making him president of operations, and offer him 40 percent of the profits as an incentive (since we never made a profit anyway). This took me out of the day-to-day decisions in the helicopter business and allowed me to focus on my primary job. Dad and I ran the helicopter business for another ten years without ever having to put in additional funds. Thanks, Dad, once again for your wisdom.

In the early stages, it was tough to run a business with only one heli-copter. Either all of my clients would want to fly at the same time or none would want to fly. We had to rent other helicopters to handle the overflow. One of our best customers was the chair and founder at Commerce Bank. He used our helicopter to find new branch locations for this fast-growing bank. He would fly over busy intersections look-ing for prime locations. Then he came to me and said, "Dirk, I really don't like it when you put me in one of the other helicopters." The ones we rented as backup to my helicopter were slower, noisier, and had poor air conditioning. He said if I didn't buy another Cabin Class A-Star, he would get one and become my competition. I asked him if he liked my helicopter, pilots, and services, and I told him I used to be a bank stock analyst, and by all accounts, he knew how to run a great regional bank, but he knew nothing about running a charter helicopter business. "So, here's the deal. You provide capital to buy a helicopter like mine and invest $250,000 as working capital. Put in another $100,000 because you like me and I am so good looking, and you will own 49 percent because I want you to have nothing to do with operations." He agreed to everything, except the hundred grand for my good looks. Actually, he did come up with $50,000, so I said he didn't fully appreciate my good looks.

On a side note, my chief pilot was flying the Commerce Bank founder into Manhattan on the morning of 9/11. They had just flown past the Statue of Liberty and were halfway across the Hudson River when the explosions in the World Trade Center happened. Somehow, my pilot, after witnessing what he thought was an accident, landed on the Thirty-Fourth Street heliport on the East River. FEMA immediately commandeered my pilot for three days of non-stop flights between Newark and Manhattan to support the rescue efforts and supply critical services to Manhattan. Once things settled down, FEMA asked me to submit a bill for the pilot's time and helicopter fuel—it amounted to more than $30,000. However, as a patriot, there was no way I was going to submit the invoice. Covering these expenses was the least I could do for our country in this time of need.

Anyway, had it not been for my father's overwhelming support and belief, I would have never been able to experience the thrill of building a chartered helicopter business. Dad's support spoke volumes about him because it was just another way he was there for me throughout my life. For this and many reasons, I always felt his love for me and support of my dreams, goals, and vision. I am who I am today because of everything I learned from him—especially what I learned from his business savvy, quotes, and commitment to strategic philanthropy.

DAD'S SAYINGS

I often heard my father say: "I am the luckiest man on earth."

His belief was that life is psychosomatic. And he believed strongly in the power of positive thinking.

He did not like wasteful or spendthrift individuals. He had a clay piggy bank on his breakfast table that said: "The world smiles on savers, and frowns on spenders."

Another quote he often used after finishing a project was: "Stop gilding the lily. Good enough is good enough."

In the woodshop, when I was about to do a fine cut, difficult sanding, or apply finish coats to the furniture we made together, he would say:

"Don't boober it!" In other words, don't mess it up. He always had a way to encourage you with a challenge.

When picking lawyers to partner with, he said: "Make sure they are 'can-do' lawyers, rather than ones carrying their book of 'nos'."

Dad's admonishment to the young girls of our family in their teens was: "Don't bring home any sick puppies." Meaning, they shouldn't let their motherly instincts cause them to bring home boyfriends who needed to be fixed.

Since this was seen as sexist, Dad quickly started telling the boys: "Don't bring home any mewing kittens."

When Dad witnessed a good play in sports or achieved lofty goals, he exclaimed, "*Mirabile dictu!*" (Latin for "wonderful to relate to," but to Dad it meant "How about that?")

Dad also dedicated his life to the Eisenhower principle: "Always leave people, places, and things better than you found them."

One saying he often used referring to wealth and money was: "To those who receive much, much is expected."

In conclusion, since he was such a strong man of God, his three favorite doctrines of the Swedenborgian faith were:

- Doctrine of Use: "Doesn't matter what your station in life is, you need to be industrious and a productive member of society."

- Doctrine of Charity: "Be kind and generous."

- Doctrine of Conjugal Love: "The marriage of a woman and a man looking to God gives the promise of eternal marriage in heaven."

In relation to that first doctrine, my father would have agreed with the advice that Peter Drucker gave to Jim Collins just before he published his book *Good to Great*: "Don't worry about being successful. Worry about being useful."

My father was my greatest mentor. I loved him deeply, and I know we will be reunited in heaven one day. He was an incredible father to his seven children, and an incredible grandfather to his twenty-seven grandchildren. He lived a full and prosperous life and eventually passed away at ninety-seven. As a side note, he regularly played golf until six months before his passing, and he would often shoot his age during the last few years of his golfing prowess. In the final months of his life, I found myself standing behind him gripping the back of his belt to steady him on his fluid back swing. We all loved him, and we deeply miss him, but his legacy lives on in us!

In addition to having my dad, James Jungé, as a mentor, I was fortunate to have many others. As I write, I can hear their words of encouragement and advice.

UNCLE GARTH PITCAIRN

My mother's brother, Uncle Garth, was a shy young boy who found the works of Dale Carnegie and Stephen Covey when he grew up. These books had a profound influence on him and his effectiveness at home, in the community, and at work. My uncle encouraged me to study Dale Carnegie and his books *How to Win Friends and Influence People* and *The Leader in You.*

I thought it very cool that Uncle Garth was friends with Stephen Covey. I often ask people I am trying to get to know if they could only have two books for the rest of their life, which two would they be? My own answer is clear: *The Bible* and *The 7 Habits of Highly Effective People.* With my uncle's encouragement, I read Stephen Covey and attended many of his seminars. His teachings have made a tremendous difference in my life.

ADVISORS, CONSULTANTS, AND PEERS

The following are influential people who helped shape my unique perspective on multigeneration family systems.

- Craig E. Aronoff, PhD, along with John Ward, who was founder of the Family Business Consulting Group based in Chicago. From him I learned many helpful methods for conflict resolution and how to maintain family enterprises.

- Carolyn Bailey is a member of the Gallo family and the codeveloper of FEAT (Family Enterprise Assessment Tool) with Dennis Jaffee. As I mentioned above, FEAT is the go-to for family business surveys around the globe.

- David Bork was the founder of the Aspen Family Business Consulting Group. He is also the author of *The Little Red Book of Family Business*, which provides great insights on how to deal with numerous issues facing families. His considerable work in Turkey with leading families was instrumental in giving me a global perspective.

- Deborah Bright is the author of many books, including *The Pro-Achievement Principle*. I have learned many things from her, and she has been a great friend for many years.

- Peter Davis is a founder of the original Wharton Family Forum. From him, I learned the importance of independent directors and their fiduciary roles in sustaining family enterprises. He also introduced me to the concept of the "Family Council" as part of a family governance structure.

- François de Visscher is a shareholder and past director of his own family's global enterprise, N.V. Bekaert S.A., headquartered in Belgium and founded by his great-grandfather in 1880. He is also a leading family business consultant with Cambridge Family Enterprises Group. From him I learned the importance of providing liquidity opportunities for multiple generational families and the need for a global perspective.

- Ann Dugan is the founder of the Institute for Entrepreneurial Excellence at the Katz School of Business at the University of

Pittsburgh. She brought together 200 family owned and closely held businesses in the greater Pittsburgh area. She taught me how to put compelling family forums together.

- Sara Hamilton is the founder of the Family Office Exchange (FOX), which is a leading global consultancy for family offices. Sara taught me how important it is to learn from your peers since they have experienced the things you will likely experience. A talented networker, she connected many of us in the family office industry.

- Barbara Hauser, a prolific writer and thinker, is an outstanding attorney and family business advisor who helped Pitcairn as one of our primary independent directors over the years. She taught me how to be a better board chair, highlighted the importance of sound governance processes, and shared my journey of promoting women's roles.

- Jay Hughes taught me about the unique challenges involved in generational succession following a business founder's passing on of the family fortune. He also taught me the importance of including in-laws (married-ins) by the third generation or they might turn into the outlaws.

- Dennis Jaffee is a respected family business consultant and a professor at Saybrook. Dennis and Joe Paul were instrumental in developing an original family inventory that Pitcairn used to move the family business inventory forward as a family wealth inventory. Dennis, Carolyn Bailey, and FEAT are the standard for families desiring a complete family survey.

- Ivan Landsberg has consistently brought a global perspective to the field of family business consultancy. He taught me the importance of maintaining a bigger, broader, global perspective.

- Greg McCann is a professor and consultant at Stetson University and has made a major commitment to growing its family business studies program. He was also a major player in developing the Transition Seminar Series put on by *Family Business Magazine.*

- Dr. Eric Muten was a psychologist who taught me about incorporating theater into programs and family forums. He was a constructive partner in helping me develop as a playwright.

- Ernesto Pose is a consultant who runs the family business center Firebird University PHX. He taught me the importance of developing a curriculum for future family business leaders.

- John Ward was also a founding members of the Family Business Consulting Group in Chicago. He taught me the importance of preparing multiple individuals for future leadership positions.

- Peter White is a family business consultant who formed International Skye, the first forum for private family offices. He taught me that Pitcairn's challenges were not unique and professionals and families could benefit from a learning community. Peter spearheaded getting family offices to put together summer family boot camps for next generation leaders where peer-to-peer learning could flourish. This effort is still going today and is called The Summer Institute.

- Kathy Wiseman is a prominent family business advisor. She taught me the importance of "Bowen Theory," which stresses the need for emotional intelligence perspectives to deal with the multiple challenges facing family enterprises.

LEARNING FROM FRIENDS

The following personal and family friends have also been great teachers:

- Dick Brickman was one of my dad's closest friends. He was a great independent director at Pitcairn and taught me how to

make Pitcairn a client-centered enterprise. I learned the importance of strategic planning from him.

- Thomas Dudley Davis is a dear friend who became my older
  brother when I lost my blood older brother. Dudley taught
  me the importance of living a life of service with strong family
  values. He taught me many life lessons—and the game of golf.

- Don Freeman was a second-generation family leader and world-
  renowned trade show organizer. He taught me how to build a
  client-centered organization. Don said I always reminded him
  of his father. When I retired, I got a plaque with his father Buck
  Freeman's quote: "Nothing great was ever achieved without
  enthusiasm."

- James Olin Hutchinson is a friend I have known for years. Jim
  is a founding partner of ReGeneration Partners. He introduced
  me to the Freeman Company, a global trade show company
  where I became an independent director and the chair of their
  compensation committee.

- Ron Nelson was my gym instructor, geometry teacher, and football, wrestling, and lacrosse coach. He taught me many things,
  including respect for our military, how to create a strong work
  ethic, how to compete at the highest level, and how to persevere.

- Tony Odhner was a longtime friend. Our families enjoyed a
  close relationship over the years. He was one of the best friends
  I ever had. He didn't go to college but was one of the smartest
  people I knew. He was a renaissance man, and his knowledge
  of politics was incredible. As it turns out, he and Dudley were
  classmates. Tony was also a retired Marine.

- Clay Riddell was a geologist and partnered with my dad on
  Clay's initial public offering (IPO). He taught me how to effectively develop next generation family leaders for his enterprise

and the importance of developing a strong fiduciary board. I was also thrilled to see Dad and Clay growing old together and having great family connections. Our families have remained close and still work together. Clay's son Jim is the CEO and Chair of the company his father created, and I am honored to sit on their board.

- Marty Roark was one of my Vistage Chairs for twenty years. He was very helpful in developing my leadership abilities. His one-on-one sessions were particularly helpful in planning for my retirement and helping to develop a transition plan for my successor.

- Hans Ziegler had a background in public trust companies and investment management. As CEO of Pitcairn while I was Chair, he helped me further the professionalism of our business.

- Finally, when you list individuals and friends who influenced you, you always run the risk of not mentioning everyone you would like to mention. Therefore, my list is incomplete. Just know how fortunate I feel to have had so many friends, associates, mentors, and coaches. You have all played a key role in my development. I couldn't have done it without you. Thank you!

KEY POINTS FOR LEARNING FROM YOUR ANCESTORS AND MENTORS

1. Succession plans for family enterprises should not put all their eggs in one basket, but rather develop multiple options for key leadership positions.

2. I feel Pitcairn was fortunate when my dad married into the family and smart when they promoted him to take over key leadership positions. By doing this, they addressed another issue

I mentioned earlier—including "married-ins" in the family governance structure, as this inclusivity helps mute family conflict.

3. Family and friends can be the best mentors.

4. Learn your family history.

5. Invest in networking.

EXERCISE

1. What is the most profound wisdom you gained from your ancestors? Which ancestors taught you this?

_____

_____

_____

_____

_____

2. What were the most useful lessons you learned from mentors? Which mentors taught you these lessons?

_____

_____

_____

_____

_____

3. What wisdom have you amassed? Whom do you want to share this wisdom with? How will you communicate this wisdom to those you want to share it with?

_____

_____

_____

_____

Chapter 6

LEAVING PEOPLE, PLACES, AND THINGS
BETTER THAN YOU FOUND THEM

"Excellent firms don't believe in excellence—
only in constant improvement and constant change."

— Tom Peters

People often ask, "So, Dirk, what generation are you in the Pitcairn clan?" I say, "It depends. I'm first generation as an entrepreneur reinventing an established single family office. I'm second generation of a non-blood family leader who revitalized our champion company, PPG Industries. I'm third generation to my grandfather, who saw the wisdom to partner with his brothers in forming one of the original single family offices in the United States. And I'm fourth generation to my great-grandfather, John Pitcairn, Jr., who was a cofounder of the Pittsburgh Plate Glass Company in 1883."

GENERATION ONE

At age thirteen, my great-grandfather left school. His older brother was best friends with Andrew Carnegie who got all of his chums jobs at the Pennsylvania Railroad. While working at the railroad, John taught himself telegraphy. At the time, the railroad network was *the* business system that connected people, goods, services, and businesses physically, just like the internet does today digitally. Through that experience, Great-Grandfather saw the explosive growth of oil and gas in western

Pennsylvania. The first two oil wells in the United States were in Oil City and Pitcairn, Pennsylvania.

At seventeen, Great-Grandfather took his life savings and bought a large farm in Western Pennsylvania where his employer would have to lay tracks to shuttle employees and crude oil from the countryside to the oil refineries in downtown Pittsburgh. This gamble paid off big time. He tripled his money in six months and soon had a major network of railroad tracks going through his property. Today, this might be considered insider trading. At that time, it was just shrewd business.

Great-Grandfather was definitely an uncommon entrepreneur—his biography, written by Richard R. Gladish, was titled *John Pitcairn: Uncommon Entrepreneur*. After his initial success with real estate, he became a major independent oil and gas operator with wells on his land. He made money from the value of the land appreciating and by selling easements to the railroad.

Because at the time Standard Oil refined and marketed oil for the independent producers, it had a monopoly and set prices. The bottom line was after Standard Oil had approved a fixed price for the commodity, it cut the price in half so the independent oil producers went bankrupt and Standard Oil could purchase their properties at ten cents on the dollar. This is my own view and may not be totally accurate.

Sometime around the 1870s, the independent oil producers asked Great-Grandfather to represent them in a meeting with John D. Rockefeller and Standard Oil over contract disputes. Great-Grandfather was only five-foot-six and going to see "the man" in Cleveland, Ohio, John D. Rockefeller, who was six-foot-one, to deal with the disputed contracts. As the story goes, Great-Grandfather began the discussion on the second floor of a hotel by saying that despite both sides employing the best lawyers to resolve the conflict, "we have failed" and independent oil and gas producers were losing their livelihood, and in some cases, their lives.

Reacting to this serious statement, Rockefeller reached across the table to shake Great-Grandfather's hand and said, "I agree. This has to end." With that, Rockefeller led Great-Grandfather out to a balcony overlooking a courtyard full of media people and said to the assembled crowd, "While JP represents the other side of this dispute, representing the independent oil and gas operators with regard to pricing, he is a man of such integrity that whatever he determines to be the just resolution, I and Standard Oil will be bound by that resolution." Shortly after this historic meeting, fair contracts were written and honored for many years. The independent producers and Standard Oil thrived.

In the early 1880s, John Pitcairn, Jr. was considered one of the first technology transfer agents. He went to Europe to learn how to best manufacture glass from the British and French. Impressed by their far superior technology, he bought the North American glass manufacturing rights from the British and French. A serious, protracted recession in the US from the 1870s to the early 1880s had devastated ten glass plants up and down the Three Rivers in the Pittsburgh area. In 1883, with his new technology in hand and considerable capital from his oil and gas business, he purchased the ten glass plants for ten cents on the dollar and revitalized them, revolutionizing glass manufacturing in the US in 1883. Within ten years of launching the Pittsburgh Plate Glass Company, his organization was manufacturing 70 percent of all the glass made in the United States.

The contractors who bought glass for office buildings, warehouses, and residential housing all required paint to finish their projects. To satisfy the demand, Great-Grandfather first warehoused paint bought from other producers (similar to Lowe's or Home Depot today), but he soon began producing paint. Hence, it became the Pittsburgh Plate Glass and Paint Company.

In time, Great-Grandfather was viewed as a Renaissance man, traveling the world buying new technology and becoming a noted serial entrepreneur. Great-Grandfather competed effectively with the "Titans of Industry," all with only an eighth-grade education. By the ends of his life, his entrepreneurial skills and ability to communicate with people of all backgrounds allowed him not only to build an empire but to be fluent in six languages and to love the arts and antiquities.

THE STORY OF EVOLUTION AND CHANGE

Later in Great-Grandfather's life, his ability to multitask allowed him to manage his businesses while following his passion for his faith. He moved to downtown Philadelphia to be closer to his small Swedenborgian church. He took care of his global business operations while also present for his family and faith.

During the 1890s, Great-Grandfather went through a "vision quest" with the bishop and leading ministers of the Swedenborgian church. He said although he loved the church and its teachings, it was never going to grow if it remained city bound. He proposed a plan to buy property in the countryside, twenty-five miles north of Philadelphia, where, with the support of the bishop, a new faith-based community would be built. This community would have its own schools, government, police, and firefighters. Great-Grandfather would provide the bulk of the financing for this new community and would set out to build a cathedral.

This new faith-based community was named Bryn Athyn (Welsh for "hill of unity" or "hill of cohesion"). All these years later, many members of our families still reside there.

In the early 1900s, Pittsburgh Plate Glass Industries (PPG) added industrial chemicals to its product lines as a third leg of this Fortune 200 company. Great-Grandfather was instrumental in planning the future of the faith and also laid a solid foundation of business, philanthropy, and opportunity for future generations of his family.

As a man of great courage and resolve, John always did what was right for those who worked for him. For example, in the early 1900s when his company was producing 70 percent of US glass, he quickly expanded manufacturing into Europe. During World War I, one of his plants was in Belgium, which was occupied by the Germans, so plant employees had not been paid for six months. However, they continued to work without pay. After several failed attempts to send payroll during the occupation of Belgium, Great-Grandfather decided to take matters into his own hands. Great-Grandfather got on a ship dressed in shabby clothing. He took two large suitcases full of cash on the steamer from New York to London. Then he boarded a train to Belgium, eventually sneaking behind German lines carrying two suitcases full of cash. He made it to the plant and paid his employees' back wages, plus cash to tide them over for the following year. This is yet another example of the pure grit my great-grandfather possessed. As one of his dear friends often said, when Great-Grandpa saw something wrong, he was prepared almost immediately to do something about it.

John Pitcairn, Jr. died in 1916, when my grandfather, Raymond Pitcairn, was thirty-two. Raymond was Great-Grandfather's eldest son and a partner at a law firm in Philadelphia. Upon his father's death, he left the law practice and stepped in to represent the founding ownership block at Pittsburgh Plate Glass.

From 1916 to 1923, Great-Grandfather's three sons, Raymond, Theodore, and Harold, organized their own cadre of accountants, lawyers, tax and trust experts, and consultants. As good Scotsmen, they saw this was inefficient, so my grandfather proposed they create a single family office, thus reducing expenses to operating a single organization to take care of their collective needs, which constituted a substantial savings. The brothers pooled their assets and formed "The Pitcairn Company," which was a pioneer of single family offices in the United States. About the same time, the Rockefellers formed Rockefeller & Company and the Phipps family formed Bessemer Trust. This year, 2023, is our centennial anniversary of launching the Pitcairn Family Office in 1923.

GENERATION TWO

Even though my grandfather, Raymond Pitcairn, was extremely busy governing PPG, and he was also the chair of the Pitcairn Company. Somehow, he also found time to get involved in politics. He was credited with convincing Dwight D. Eisenhower (Ike) to seek the highest office in the land. Ike become the thirty-fourth president.

On Grandfather's seventieth birthday, Ike and Mamie Eisenhower were in attendance. I was a bold young boy who photo-bombed Ike and Mamie at this birthday celebration. A few years later, an uncle asked me to set up the hunting blinds for a crow hunt for Ike, my grandfather Raymond, and two of my uncles. My job was to take an old, battery-powered, 45 rpm record player with big speakers out to the blinds at the edge of a cornfield. The record was of screaming crows. We played it loud to attract crows.

I didn't recognize until a few years later that not everyone's grandparents had the President and First Lady as guests at their home. As I look back on it, it was one of the things I found so impressive about my grandparents—they were mindful of not allowing their grandchildren to take their position of influence and privilege for granted. They wanted their grandchildren to be raised to know the value of hard work and not feel they were superior to others.

With Great-Grandfather John's inspiration and spirit, each of his three sons followed their passion while being stewards of the family's legacy enterprises. Great-Grandfather's second son, Reverend Theodore Pitcairn, was a practicing minister in Bryn Athyn, Pennsylvania. From the very beginning of the Pitcairn family office in 1923, Raymond, Theodore, and Harold Pitcairn were all on the board of the Pitcairn Company, representing the needs of their branch of the family. Theodore became a world-renowned collector of impressionist art. His collection included works by Monet, Van Gogh, Pissarro, and Renoir. One of his most recognized pieces, Monet's *La terrasse à Sainte-Adresse*, now hangs in the Metropolitan Museum of Art. You can see a photo of this painting below.

Monet's *La terrasse à Sainte-Adresse*.

John Pitcairn, Jr.'s youngest son, Harold Pitcairn, was only eighteen when his father died. He was almost single-mindedly dreaming of aviation. Today, he is recognized as one of the first true aviators in the US. By the time he was six, he was designing and creating perfect hand-made gliders. His early designs would serve him well in designing the future aircraft. Harold Pitcairn served as a pilot in the Army Air Corp. Shortly after World War I ended, he purchased many surplus aircraft (many had been used in World War I). He refurbished these and won the first federal contract for flying cancelled checks from Newark to Atlanta and on to Miami. This was the beginning of one of the first airmail services in the US. As these early aircraft proved to be unreli-able and accident prone, Harold Pitcairn began designing the Pitcairn Mail wing—heavy-duty bi-planes with big, powerful radial engines and storage nose cones for carrying large volumes of mail.

Some people knew the flight schedule and that there was room for a passenger or two. Captain Eddie Rickenbacker joined Harold Pitcairn's mail services venture, and together they formed Eastern Transportation, which later became Eastern Airlines. With Rickenbacker focused on passengers at the expense of freight and airmail, Harold Pitcairn de-cided to leave Eastern Airlines, even though his passion for aviation was still alive and well.

Harold Pitcairn had heard about an inventive genius in Spain, Juan de la Cierva, who had the idea to take a free-wheeling rotor system on top of a stubby winged plane, thus creating the first short takeoff and landing aircraft (also called a STOL). Like his father who had purchased technology rights from the French and British for making glass, Harold Pitcairn purchased the rights to manufacture the Pitcairn-Cierva (STOL) from de la Cierva.

The Pitcairn-Cierva main rotor system used a vertical shaft that al-lowed the rotor system to be titled and changed in a horizontal plane. It was later used in the first helicopters.

At the end of World War II, the US government was responsible for restoring the licenses and patents of those who had pooled their resources to defend the country. But they ignored the rights and patents to Harold Pitcairn's autogiro and its significance in creating the modern helicopter. This allowed Boeing, Sikorsky, Bell, Hughes, and Schweizer to produce helicopters without compensation to Harold Pitcairn.

Harold Pitcairn was a true patriot who essentially gave up his major airport (today Willow Grove Naval Air Station) for the war effort. It is almost unthinkable that he had to sue the US government to restore his patents. Uncle Harold Pitcairn died in the early 1960s having dissipated most of his wealth by fighting a lawsuit that lasted years and years. Harold's two older brothers decided to take up the fight for their brother and his heirs. Being thrifty, instead of paying huge fees to a law firm, they put the patent attorney and his litigation team on staff at the Pitcairn Company. Finally, in 1971, the biggest patent infringement suit against the US government came to an end, with the estate of Harold Pitcairn coming out on top. Today, more than 300 family members are beneficiaries of the trust set up with the lawsuit's proceeds.

As part of the settlement, Pitcairn brought expert testimony to get the interest penalty on the award changed from 2 to 6 percent. This required an act of Congress. It is a sad commentary that the government fought a twenty-seven-year battle that only a family of substantial means could withstand to avoid righting a wrong that was entirely their fault. Over years, five federal judges hearing the suit died.

John Pitcairn, Jr. also had an amazing daughter, Vera, who was very passionate about becoming a teacher. But sadly, she died at eighteen due to a ruptured appendix.

After the Pitcairn Company was established, my grandfather focused on achieving his father's dream of building a cathedral for their church.

Because it had been his long-term dream, Great-Grandfather had taken my grandfather on many trips to assemble a collection of antiquities and art brought back to the construction site to inspire the artisans building the cathedral with century-old cathedral construction processes and designs.

The collection featured eleventh and twelfth century stained glass, Roman and Greek statuary, medieval weapons for the metal workers, Italian and Spanish wood carvings for the woodworkers, and Roman stone arches, columns, and capitals for the stonecutters. These artifacts were all on pedestals on the construction site to inspire the hundred-plus workers to achieve the look and feel of cathedrals built by the old masters in Europe.

Many of the refinements of European cathedrals included subtleties in the curvature of the walls and pillars, so Grandfather made sure he had the same lines and curves in his designs.

At one point, Great-Grandfather and Grandfather Pitcairn had hired a leading architect, but after his father's death, my grandfather had a falling out with the architect, who kept saying, "Mr. Pitcairn, you keep talking about all the great things you want this building to achieve. Your church (note he didn't say cathedral) is going to be too small and only the great cathedrals of Europe could achieve what you are envisioning."

Grandfather released the architect and became the architect of record for the cathedral. As he was not trained, he did everything with scale models. In the woods behind the Bryn Athyn Cathedral, stone archways were erected so he could find the optimum design of key features while walking through them in nature.

The primary construction was between 1916 and 1929, and only the foundation was laid between 1913-1916. After Great-Grandfather's passing in 1916, Grandfather Pitcairn went full-steam ahead for the next thirteen years to finish the construction and realize his father's dream.

As a result of this achievement, Raymond Pitcairn became the only person ever on the board of the American Institute of Architects who wasn't a formerly trained architect. Today, the Bryn Athyn Cathedral is the proud center of a Federally Identified Historic District, which also features the family's historic homes.

One of Great-Grandfather's dreams was to create an educational system based on Swedenborgian teachings. Today, the Bryn Athyn Church School has a kindergarten through eighth grade elementary school. The Academy of the New Church contains boys and girls' schools, Bryn Athyn College, and a theological school.

GENERATION THREE

In 1955, at seventy, Raymond Pitcairn had created the family office bringing the Pitcairn brothers together and he was director at PPG. He had been grooming his eldest son, Nathan, to take over leadership of the broader and rapidly expanding family. Tragically, his eldest son died of cancer.

Raymond Pitcairn turned to his son-in-law, James Jungé (my father), who had an extensive background in industrial production and was operating a successful consulting firm working with major oil refineries and petrochemical plants in the US and the Caribbean. He had also developed an extensive network of investment bankers because his consulting clients often needed substantial financing.

Dad was very successful in his own right. He had the experience required to lead the next generation of the Pitcairn enterprise and, importantly, revitalize PPG Industries.

Dad often said one of the things he liked most about consulting was being paid to "case the joint." Grandfather asked his two younger sons, who were my dad's tennis buddies, to try to convince him to work for the Pitcairn Company. Dad turned them down, saying, "That is your stuff. I have got my own business and life to live."

Grandfather invited Dad to his home—a ten-story castle with a tower named Glencairn. Dad was a bit intimidated getting into the elevator to meet Grandfather and wondering what the old bird wanted from him.

Grandfather said, "I understand you have consistently rejected the notion of coming to work for the Pitcairn family."

"Yes, sir," Dad replied.

"Don't you understand with our core investment in PPG and the growing services of the Pitcairn Company, your background is ideally suited to be our next leader?"

"Sir," replied my father, "the need was not previously expressed. If you need me, I will be there."

That was the beginning of Dad's (James Jungé's) influence on the transformation of PPG and the Pitcairn Family Office.

Dad was only thirty-four and understood he was the new kid and the youngest on the block, so he committed to a gradual shift to gain acceptance of his leadership. Dad understood this opportunity would require 100 percent of his time and focus, so he divested all his previous business interests, selling to his previous partners.

At the time, Pitcairn still owned more than 50 percent of PPG Industries' shares. This was by far the most important investment owned by the Pitcairn family, their trusts, and related charities. Dad was also an active lay leader in church governance, specifically over the endowments of the numerous church charities and professionalized their investments.

Job one for Dad was to focus on revitalizing Pittsburgh Plate Glass Company and improving the performance of its stock. In the mid-1950s, PPG was seen as a "conglomerate pig" by Wall Street. The stock was depressed and investors were losing value. During his first three years on the PPG board, Dad completed a dramatic turnaround of PPG's prospects.

Dad was in a position to revitalize the board of directors, the management team, and the physical plant and equipment. His plan for doing this was called the "Blueprint for the Future."

As the banks and equity markets declined to provide the capital to fund this turnaround, Dad went old school by cutting dividends in half to raise the capital to fund the turnaround internally. The turnaround was going to be a ten-year plan, but within five years, PPG had become a Wall Street darling.

Understanding the importance of diversification, Dad then built an investment team at the Pitcairn Company that would manage diversification and the fund of the holding company by selling a portion of the Pitcairn PPG block.

In the 1960s to 1980s, Dad sold blocks of PPG to the public, thus providing additional capital to continue the diversification program he built. Dad's plan included investments in a broad list of publicly traded companies, real estate, oil and gas, coal, railroads, and many venture capital opportunities. Under Dad's leadership, Pitcairn became a well-recognized institutional investor.

Once again, the importance of an entrepreneurial spirit as one of the few antidotes to the shirtsleeves to shirtsleeves in three generations phenomenon is apparent in this story.

During Dad's leadership at Pitcairn, we had what appeared to be the perfect nuclear family (the Ozzie and Harriet type). But we faced the tragic loss of my eldest brother, Jan, due to drugs, alcohol, and a dysfunctional marriage. It was a heavy burden for the whole family. To this day, we still love and miss him, as do many others. Being the closest to my brother, I felt I surely could have prevented this tragedy. I have had to do some heavy introspection over the years with professional help to deal with Jan's loss.

In the early 1980s, the city of Pittsburgh witnessed the devastation of leveraged buyouts (LBOs) and investors ripping the heart out of the downtown. Pittsburgh had more corporate headquarters at the time than any other US city. This situation, coupled with the mismanagement of downtown real estate, led to a decaying city center.

PPG, being a significant corporate partner in the city, wanted to show the community they would be a permanent part of the revitalization of downtown Pittsburgh. They hired Phillip Johnson, a world-renowned architect, to develop a corporate headquarters complex whose footprint would encompass three city blocks. My dad recalls an important PPG board meeting where Johnson revealed his concept for the new HQ. With great fanfare, Johnson pushed a draped cart into the boardroom. In doing his homework on PPG, he spent time studying the John Pitcairn, Jr. archives and was struck by the beauty of the Bryn Athyn Cathedral. Moving the cart into the center of the boardroom, Johnson grabbed the peak of the drape and yanked it off, revealing a gothic style, all glass building resembling the Bryn Athyn Cathedral. Half of the board recoiled while the other half leaned in with smiles on their faces.

PPG Industries corporate headquarters

Johnson was in his early eighties at the time and very proud of his architectural prowess. My father recalls him saying, "I have just witnessed a varied response to my commissioned work. It was made clear to me that my charge was to make a statement for PPG and its city. I can tell you, should you vote to approve this plan, it will do for Pittsburgh what the Tour d'Eiffel did for Paris."

The design was approved and this gothic sibling to the Bryn Athyn Cathedral became John Pitcairn's legacy and contribution to the Pittsburgh skyline. If you drive through Pittsburgh, you can't miss it because it is unique. These three blocks became a key part of the downtown Pittsburgh revitalization, featuring retail shops, restaurants, a major office tower, and a winter garden with an ice-skating rink.

To top off PPG's commitment to Pittsburgh, PPG Paint Arena is now the home of the NHL's Pittsburgh Penguins.

PITCAIRN AVOIDS THE LETHARGY WITNESSED AT PPG

Early on, my dad put together a leadership succession plan at Pitcairn and he quickly installed my thirty-eight-year-old cousin as president.

A few years later, my father was misdiagnosed with the flu when, in fact, he had a ruptured appendix. He developed peritonitis, an often deadly condition known to follow a ruptured appendix. It basically poisons your body from the inside. My father was in critical condition in intensive care for six weeks. During his hospitalization, four of my uncles on the board of the Pitcairn Company, who were directors and trustees of the majority of the family assets, got together and decided my cousin was no longer fit to be president. Advice from council was to call an interim election and have a vote of "no confidence."

My cousin's abrupt departure from the company caused a major schism in the broader Pitcairn family. It seemed to be the first time the family was not in harmony. On Dad's return, he had to deal with the fallout from the split. The Pitcairns, being no different than most families, faced real-life challenges. Today, almost fifty years later, some family turmoil still exists over this cousin's abrupt departure from the company and the aftermath.

GENERATION FOUR—MOVING FROM PATRIARCHAL TO MORE DEMOCRATIC AND INCLUSIVE

I graduated from Lehigh University in 1971 with a degree in economics and finance. Summer internships in Pitcairn's investment department during high school and college ensured my degree gave me the requisite background to pursue a career as an investment professional.

One week after graduation, I married my high school sweetheart and moved back to Bryn Athyn, Pennsylvania. I chose to apply at Provident

National Bank because it was considered one of the best investment management firms in the Philadelphia area. I was offered a position in their trust and investment division, where I was a portfolio manager and research analyst. I was soon promoted to trust officer.

Five years later, in 1976, I was in preliminary discussions with Goldman Sachs in New York City. When the head of the Pitcairn investment department heard this news, he approached me and said, "We need help in portfolio management, securities research, and on the trading desk, so the time has come for you to work for us." As CEO and chair of Pitcairn, my dad had developed a leadership style that included empowering his direct reports to make decisions. So, he was not consulted, and I began my lifelong career commitment to the Pitcairn enterprise. While I could have chosen other firms, choosing Pitcairn has been one of the best decisions of my life.

The best part of a family enterprise is the *family*, and the most challenging or worst part of a family or enterprise is the *family*! When things are good, they are really good, and when they are bad, they are horrid.

A year after my cousin was let go from Pitcairn, out of ninety people on staff, I was the only fourth generation Pitcairn there. My uncles, who were family trustees and on the Pitcairn board, heard about a program at the Wharton School, the University of Pennsylvania's business school, called the Wharton Family Forum. It was one of the first forums of its type in the country. My uncles picked me to be Pitcairn's representative. This assignment was instrumental in my learning the importance of leadership and the elements of sustaining the family enterprise. Many of the approaches and philosophies I teach today go back to my experience at Wharton. It was there I first heard of the benefits of employing a family council to help govern a family business or enterprise.

Nepotism is a sensitive subject inherent to a family business or enterprise. I didn't want people thinking I was only where I was because my father was the chair. I always ensured I was qualified or overqualified for any promotion I accepted. Since I came through the investment operation, I challenged myself to become the first Chartered Financial Analyst (CFA) at Pitcairn. It was equivalent to having a doctorate in investment. Having graduated from Lehigh with honors and achieved a CFA, no one should question my credentials—at least, that was how I saw it.

One of my primary goals as I progressed in leadership positions was to keep everyone happy. Previously, my father and uncles only had fifteen adult family members to please. Now, there were a hundred-plus and growing adult family members. These numbers called for a new approach, which was partly up to me to implement. With the Wharton Family Forum experience, I was in a better position to navigate these challenges.

As a result of my cousin's departure, factions formed and many wanted to liquidate their interests and cash out. About three years after his departure, a substantial change in US tax policy allowed a holding company to liquidate before December 31, 1986, without paying capital gains tax at both the corporation and individual shareholder levels.

This change offered an incentive to liquidate our sixty-three-year-old personal holding company so dissatisfied family shareholders could cash out at an acceptable price and provide the remaining shareholders a unique opportunity to tailor investment programs to meet the growing, diverse needs of the Pitcairn family.

In the end, after considerable analysis, we decided to liquidate the personal holding company, which required the sale of almost all of the assets, including the family's PPG stock. For the first time, the Pitcairn family separated itself from the company it had founded.

We were now entering the third phase of Pitcairn. The first two had been the global businesses of PPG prior to 1923, and the single family office from 1923 to 1986. In 1987, the third phase began when the family office reconstituted itself as a private trust company, Pitcairn Trust Company, located in the Philadelphia suburb of Jenkintown, PA. Instead of managing only the family's money, the trust company would manage outside clients' funds as well. Today, Pitcairn serves a hundred-plus multigenerational families around the world in addition to the Pitcairn family.

Statistics show less than 5 percent of successful first-generation family businesses are intact by the fourth generation. A lot of people think this is due to bad decisions. Either they over-leverage themselves or pick the wrong products. Some blame poor tax planning. But, in fact, the main reason is the family forgets how to be a family and communicate effectively. We had just reconfirmed our decision to be a family business, even if some family members had chosen to leave. We were stronger now for having refocused our purpose.

When we reformed, I was chosen to lead the new family business. How that happened I'll explain in more detail in Chapter 8. Suffice to say, the Bryn Athyn Cathedral was an example in our family of a son completing a father's dream. Now I was completing my father's dream of seeing me lead the transition from a successful single family office to a thriving world-class multi-family enterprise.

Today, when people ask me how our family got through the generational transitions and stayed together, I say forming a single-family office in the second generation helped. And the fact that the Pitcairn family used long-term, multigenerational trusts to transfer the wealth was also helpful. We were one of the first families to use a family council in our governance structure. Pitcairn has also maintained an entrepreneurial approach to the future. And finally, a majority of the John

Pitcairn, Jr. clan were and are members of a small religious community, called Swedenborgians, and involved with its charities.

KEY POINTS FOR LEAVING PEOPLE, PLACES, AND THINGS BETTER THAN YOU FOUND THEM

1. Families fight, so a strong governance structure is essential to keeping family enterprises and businesses together and avoiding poor decisions based on disagreements.

2. Trusts are a must in transmitting generational wealth.

3. Multigenerational family operations allow for long-term planning since projects can straddle generations.

4. Diversify—all investments have cycles. You're working on sustaining the core, not preserving each piece.

5. "To whom much is given, much will be required." (Luke 12:48)

6. Anonymous quote: "Some people make your day better; some people make your life better."

EXERCISE

1. Who is most important in your life? Whose life do you want to make better because you can?

_____

_____

_____

_____

_____

_____

2. Which places in the world nurture your soul?

_____

_____

_____

_____

_____

_____

_____

_____

_____

_____

3. Which projects do you want to complete to make life better for yourself and/or others?

_____

_____

_____

_____

_____

PART II:

INVESTING IN PERSONAL AND ORGANIZATIONAL DEVELOPMENT

"If you empty your purse into your head, no one can take it away from you. An investment in knowledge always pays the best interest."

— Benjamin Franklin

Chapter 7

REINVENTING THE FAMILY DYNASTY

"The story began with a single, starving family, hunted and alone on the plains of Mongolia—and ends with Kublai Khan ruling an empire larger than that of Alexander the Great or Julius Caesar. Over just three generations, that is simply the greatest rags-to-riches tale in human history."

— Conn Iggulden

REINVENTING A FAMILY DYNASTY

Below is an article by Dennis T. Jaffe, Joseph Paul, and myself published in the winter 2004 issue of *Family Business Magazine*. With permission, I have included this article in its entirety because it summarizes exactly what I am trying to encourage you to do.

> After more than a century, the Pitcairn heirs hang together by shifting their focus to their private trust company.
>
> The odds against a family sustaining a wealth-generating financial engine for more than a generation or two are staggering. When a family dynasty sells its company and sets out as a financial family in new investment directions, the odds against sustaining the same level of wealth generation are even greater. Yet five generations after the founding of what is now PPG Industries, Philadelphia's Pitcairn family is leveraging its wealth by creating

a new vehicle that seeks to sustain a high rate of return for generations to come.

Given their druthers, most fifth-generation heirs without a family company would just as soon go their separate ways and do their own thing. But by sticking together, the 200-some heirs of John Pitcairn enjoy important financial benefits, not to mention a resource network that wouldn't otherwise be available to them.

The Pitcairn family legacy stems from John Pitcairn (1841-1916), a Scottish immigrant who co-founded Pittsburgh Plate Glass Company in 1883. By the turn of the twentieth century, the company produced 70 percent of the plate glass made in America. Over the years, the renamed PPG Industries flourished, and the Pitcairn family shareholders were rewarded.

Seven years after their father's death, John's three sons—Raymond, Theodore, and Harold—formed The Pitcairn Company, a family office to look after the financial affairs of the estate and maintain voting control of PPG while they pursued other careers. Raymond represented the family interests at PPG and was engaged in building the Swedenborgian Bryn Athyn Cathedral outside Philadelphia. Theodore was passionate about the arts and pursued a career in the ministry. Harold, a lifelong aviation enthusiast, founded an airmail service that eventually led to the formation of Eastern Airlines and helped develop the Pitcairn Autogiro, a precursor to the helicopter.

Each of John Pitcairn's three sons had nine children, and by 1950, there were sixty-one descendants of the founder. In the 1960s, the family office formalized an investment department to meet the needs of the rapidly growing family. The family office also pioneered the creation of several important programs for its family shareholders: an annual report, an annual meeting, and educational programs for the children.

By its fiftieth anniversary in 1973, the Pitcairn family office had grown to more than $200 million in assets—this after paying out more than $750 million in dividends. While the returns from the family's large stake in PPG produced much of this wealth, it was time for the family to look for more dynamic and diversified investment vehicles.

Then as now, the Pitcairn heirs pursued a diverse variety of careers. They are contractors, doctors, artists, musicians, videographers, photographers, and teachers, as well as environmental scientists, psychotherapists, massage therapists, investment advisors, real estate developers, and venture capitalists. Some family members wanted to withdraw their money or manage their own investments. After considerable analysis, a decision was made to liquidate the personal holding company, which required the sale of almost all of the assets, including the family's PPG stock. For the first time, the Pitcairn family separated itself from the company it had founded. In 1987, the family office reconstituted itself as a private trust company, Pitcairn Trust Company, located in the Philadelphia suburb of Jenkintown, PA. Instead of managing only the family's money, the trust company would manage outside clients' funds as well.

This strategy represented a huge paradigm shift for the family. In making it, the Pitcairns followed the lead of other large private family offices, such as Bessemer Trust, Rockefeller, and Glenmede Trust, which had followed a similar path.

Why did the Pitcairn heirs decide to transform their private family office into a multi-client wealth management firm? For one thing, it would improve their ability to attract and retain quality professionals on the staff. Ownership could now be shared with management. And bringing non-Pitcairn family clients into the mix—with their ability to "vote with their feet" if they don't get results—would exert additional discipline on the staff that the captive family members themselves lacked the leverage to impose. Above all, the family perceived the trust company as an opportunity to vastly expand the family assets.

No more than three members of the Pitcairn family have ever actually worked at Pitcairn Trust Company at any one time. So as part of the transition to a multi-client family office, the Pitcairn heirs worked out a governance structure that reflected several clear desires: They wanted continual feedback about the business, they wanted to ensure that younger generations would participate, and they wanted the new business initiative to be guided by a "Mission and Principles" document.

Working with the family business consultant Peter Davis of the University of Pennsylvania's Wharton School, they collected ideas from about ninety family members.

The key concerns of family members soon emerged:

- Defining the limits of trustee control.

- Succession planning for family trustees.

- Determining the role of family directors.

- Ensuring family representation on the company board.

- Developing a written description of the key duties of senior officers of the corporation.

- Maintaining an ongoing "free association" policy that would allow family members and their trusts to withdraw their funds and obtain services elsewhere if they chose.

The family governance structure they designed called for two boards. The traditional Pitcairn Trust board of directors consists of ten family directors and four non-family directors. (The current board represents three generations of Pitcairn family members—two members of the third generation, seven from the fourth generation, and one from the fifth generation.) They also created a "director emeritus" status, which helped establish openings for new family board members without discarding talent of long-standing members.

But the unique feature of this governance structure was the creation of a parallel family "auxiliary board." Through a variety of tasks—like convening a family meeting every two years and overseeing a financial education program for family members—this auxiliary board functions as a continuing training ground for future family leaders, either blood relatives or their spouses.

"The problem was that as the family grew, young people didn't have the tools to step into the director role," recalls Rick Pitcairn, an investment manager and, at age forty-two, the fourth-generation head of the auxiliary board. "We thought: Why don't we have a board for the younger people, to educate them about what we do and why?"

The auxiliary board in effect became a springboard for relatives like Chris Kerr, a venture capitalist, who at age thirty-six has advanced to become the only fifth-generation member on Pitcairn Trust Company's official board. "Growing up in Bryn Athyn," he recalls, "I was intrigued by the family's business." He first got involved in 1980, when as a thirteen-year-old he attended a workshop over three weekends that was offered to introduce young people to the family's financial business. When the auxiliary board was formed, he volunteered to join.

The auxiliary board's members (currently eleven) nominate themselves, usually from the ranks of young relatives who have attended the periodic family investment and financial services seminars sponsored by the auxiliary board. These weeklong events were designed to de-mystify the financial services industry and the challenges of inherited wealth. (The seminars usually involve outside speakers as well as a trip to Wall Street.)

Another key cornerstone was the Pitcairn Trust's "free association" policy, which meant that a family member could freely decide to leave the new Trust Company. Over the years, about half of the family members have decided to leave the firm. At the end of 1993, a large group of family members left—either to pursue different investment philosophies, or because they objected to opening the Trust Company's doors to non-family clients. This difficult transition required sensitive attention to the needs and voices of all family members.

In 1998, the family office marked its seventy-fifth anniversary, and family members and the auxiliary board seized this opportunity to celebrate the past and explore the future with a special family retreat in the summer of 1999. (Relatives paid their own travel and most lodging expenses, but Pitcairn Trust paid for the events and activities.) By this time Pitcairn Trust had successfully evolved from a private single-family office serving the needs of only the Pitcairn family to one of the nation's most highly regarded full-service wealth management institutions, with more than $2 billion under management, more than half of which belongs to some 200 non-family clients.

Yet with a dramatic growth in the number of family members, the Pitcairn family's per capita wealth was in danger of decreasing unless the family found other ways to generate wealth. The stock market was booming at the time, and a new wave of high-tech millionaires was demanding more sophisticated financial planning and advice. Pitcairn Trust's managers saw an opportunity to solicit this market aggressively, but such a strategy would require a greater degree of risk. It was important to get feedback from the Pitcairn family shareholders before moving ahead. The retreat seemed like a good opportunity.

The challenge was how to listen to all the different voices in a growing family and to focus the concerns into a dialogue that would lead to effective decisions. "It has always been difficult to get all the members of a large family to give input," says Rick Pitcairn, chair of the auxiliary board that planned the retreat.

To identify everyone's concerns, the family used the "Aspen Family Wealth Inventory." This survey asks a hundred questions about the family relations and wealth management. The results provide a quick graphic "snapshot" of a family's strengths, weaknesses, and areas of disagreement (www.aspenfamilybusiness.com). By filling out the survey, family members felt assured that their concerns would be heard. Ultimately, nearly a hundred Pitcairn family members took the survey. "They saw it as an opportunity to talk back to the family and the business," Rick Pitcairn remarks.

In June 1999, 108 adult Pitcairn family members gathered for the retreat at the Sagamore resort in upstate New York. It started with a welcoming reception on a beautiful terrace overlooking Lake George. Family members were able to reunite with others who had traveled from many parts of the U.S. and Canada. The formal meeting started the next morning in the resort conference center. Pitcairn Trust chairman Dirk Jungé, a great-grandson of John Pitcairn, presided over the business meeting, which started by honoring the past in a special video. Alvin Clay, the non-family president of Pitcairn Trust, presented the firm's strategic plan to generate new wealth for the family by expanding the company's wealth management services.

After a day of activities designed for family bonding—including a scavenger hunt that divided the family into two teams—the relatives spent several hours in a formal discussion of the survey results and explored several key concerns among all business families. For example:

1. In matters of money and status, how do we ensure that the self-interest of more powerful individuals stays balanced with the family's common interests?

2. As our numbers continue to grow, how do we manage the diversity of beliefs, opinions, and values that will naturally emerge?

3. In our busy lives, how can we give our shared interests the attention they need?

4. How can we ensure that everyone is acknowledged for his or her contributions to the greater good of the family?

5. To what degree is the Trust Company obliged to ensure that individual family members will be adequately prepared for their respective lives?

6. How can we be assured that the best people are in the most responsible jobs in our company?

7. Do we need clearer policies about how individual family members grow into family leadership?

8. Just how well defined do our policies need to be concerning how our assets are valued, bought, and sold?

9. Do we need to better define the respective responsibilities of the family compared to those of the board of trustees?

10. What is the responsibility, if any, of the larger family when a relative doesn't seem able to handle the individual responsibilities and emotional challenges of wealth?

The family members were divided into discussion groups based on age (sixty-plus, fifties, forties, etc.). After discussing these questions, each age group selected a representative to speak to the entire family on behalf of the group. After all the groups had spoken, the family board members were asked to move their chairs into the center of the ballroom, form a circle, and confer with one another (in front of the whole group) about what they had just heard and what they felt their next steps needed to be.

"The discussion was wide open, passionate," recalls Chris Kerr. "People said what they felt, which lifted a lot of weight off our chests. There are some very different nuclear families, value systems, and ways of acting, even in our family group. This discussion gave us the opportunity to understand all of this, and trust that the board would listen and act in the best interests of the shareholders."

The by-product of this sort of dialogue may be just as important as the product. "The least financially informed people in a family tend to be the most skeptical," says Rick Pitcairn, who manages money for other high-net-worth clients. "Once you educate them a bit about why decisions are made, they become more comfortable." The real question for the owners is whether Pitcairn Trust could become the family's next PPG Industries. Stay tuned.

That gathering was a watershed of sorts, infusing the Pitcairn family with a renewed entrepreneurial spirit, a wealth-building focus they hadn't known for some time. One example: Two young family members, working through the auxiliary board, designed and demonstrated a beta version of an Internet family tree website, called "Relativity," to promote family exchange and communication. Each family member would be able to maintain his or her personal data, including a picture, address, and contact information.

The website also fosters the formation of affinity groups—for example, family members can search for others who share their interest in rock climbing, aviation, fishing, and scuba diving trips, Habitat for Humanity outings, whatever. Similar searches also allow networking on career decisions (searchable by company, industry, or job title), and education (searchable by school, major/minor, and degree).

"Relativity" is still evolving—a new version for the family's use is planned for the coming year. If this family networking tool can be marketed to other far-flung families, it could potentially generate new royalty income for future generations of Pitcairns.

Dennis T. Jaffe, PhD is a family business consultant in San Francisco, where he is a professor at Saybrook Graduate School and a member of the Aspen Family Business Group. Dirk Jungé is chairman of Pitcairn Trust Company. Joseph Paul is a family business consultant in Portland, Oregon, and a member of the Aspen Family Business Group.

Do family businesses make good investments?

To diversify their holdings, in 1986 the Pitcairn heirs jointly sold their entire block of PPG Industries shares back to PPG Industries at a premium over the market price. The question then became: Where to invest the proceeds? Since PPG had served the Pitcairn family so well for so long, the heirs were inclined to put at least some of their assets to work in the same way the Pitcairn family's own wealth had been cultivated: in family-controlled (albeit publicly traded) companies.

In the late 1980s, Pitcairn Trust commissioned a Wharton School study to identify and analyze a broad sample of public companies with at least 10 percent family ownership. The researchers compared those 132 companies' performance to the S&P 500 over a twenty-year period. The results were striking: The family firms significantly outperformed the S&P 500 index in bull and bear markets alike.

Within this universe of family firms, the Wharton analysts sifted through company financial reports to find the hallmarks of managerial discipline: low debt, good cash flow, reinvested earnings, thoughtful capital spending, and strong profit margins. The result was a portfolio of twenty-five to thirty stocks in which Pitcairn Trust took an investment stake—a registered investment strategy called "Family Heritage."

This portfolio performed well until 1994-95, when it lagged behind the overall market. In 1996, Pitcairn's investment professionals refined the research. Using analytical software that wasn't available when the portfolio was first established, they examined 250 prospective selections more closely for return trends, risks, and other elements. Many of the original stocks stayed in the portfolio, some were reweighted, and a number of large-cap company names were added.

Pitcairn's research has concluded that family money enjoys the big advantage of being patient money. These companies are committed to higher levels of internal reinvestment and focus on industry leadership, greater return on assets and equity—and consequently, they're superior investments.

The performance of Pitcairn's Family Heritage portfolio confirms its premise—that well-run family-controlled companies can be excellent investments over the long run.

LIFE-CHANGING LESSONS TO BUILD A DYNASTY

Few leaders throughout American history better portray what it means to change and learn during challenging times than Abraham Lincoln. Often, this type of leadership can lead to a dynasty in politics, the community, and business. On July 1, 2022, *The Epoch Times* published "32 Life-Changing Lessons to Learn from Abraham Lincoln." The complete article is posted on their website, but here is a list of these thirty-two lessons:

1. Strive to become all life created you to be.

2. Leave nothing for tomorrow that can be done today.

3. Whatever you are is good.

4. Your happiness is your responsibility.

5. Prepare and someday your chance will come.

6. Allow things to take their natural course.

7. The best way to predict your future is to create it.

8. Success can be achieved by everyone.

9. It's not the years in your life that count. It's the life in your years.

10. Strive to be worthy of recognition.

11. Better to be a little nobody than an evil somebody.

12. Character is like a tree, and reputation is its shadow.

13. Live with integrity.

14. Truth is your truest friend.

15. Do well and you will feel good. Do bad and you will feel bad.

16. Strive to be too big to take offense and too noble to give it.

17. Never give up.

18. A house divided against itself cannot stand.

19. Look for the bad in people and you surely will find it.

20. If you don't like someone, get to know them better.

21. You destroy your enemies when you make them your friends.

22. To ease another's heartache is to forget one's own.

23. If you have no friends, you have no pleasure.

24. No law can give us the right to do what is wrong.

25. An evil tree cannot bring forth good fruit.

26. If you want to test someone's character, give them power.

27. You cannot help people permanently by doing for them.

28. Those who deny freedom to others don't deserve it for themselves.

29. There is nothing good in war except its ending.

30. No man is poor who has a godly mother.

31. God is always right.

32. Better to remain silent and be thought a fool than to speak out and remove all doubt.

ALLOWING THE "MISSION" TO BECOME THE DYNASTY

The following fable from Aesop illustrates well the advantage of allowing the mission to become the dynasty for a family business or enterprise.

A person who was near death summoned their children to give them some parting advice. They gave the children a bundle of sticks and told the eldest to break it. The eldest strained with all his might, but could not break the sticks. The others tried and failed as well. Then, their parent said, "Untie the bundle, and each of you take one stick. Now, break it." When the sticks broke easily, the elderly parent said, "You see my meaning. Union gives strength."

While only a fable, that story is pertinent to all families. One family enterprise has become one of America's most extraordinary for its vision and strength of purpose. It is a family enterprise that began a century ago and with a man who had a mission. His name was John Pitcairn, Jr. His mission: to devote the fruits of his labor and his enterprise to the service of God and preserve the sacred resources God granted us. He passed that mission on to his three sons and they, in turn, passed it on to the third and fourth generation, where I come in. My generation is currently involved in passing it on to the fifth and sixth generations.

This mission's success is not measured in years or even in a single lifetime. It is measured over the generations, and it continues to this day.

Today, Pitcairn is celebrating its hundredth anniversary as a family office. The Pitcairn Family now serve a hundred-plus multigenerational families from all over the globe.

KEY POINTS FOR REINVENTING THE FAMILY DYNASTY

1. Get feedback from all the family members.

2. Establish shared goals and interests for the future of the family business.

3. If need be, liquify family holdings so family members no longer onboard can go their separate ways and the business can then be reinvented.

4. Identify those of the younger generation committed to ensure the family business/dynasty.

5. Think about the bigger picture—how can your family story be a model for other families and their family businesses?

6. Remember, it is important to develop a "committed mindset." Each generation needs to be encouraged to find their passion and then decide how to apply that passion to the family enterprise.

7. Although the current generation is responsible for providing ongoing educational and orientation programs to the broader family, make sure the next generation is involved in generating the curriculum. Ensure entrepreneurism is part of the family history. Honoring the past gives purpose to the future.

8. The invitation to include the next generation in family gatherings needs to start early and be repeated often. Study past transitions for clues as to how to manage current transitions smoothly. And make sure membership in the clan has its privileges and people are proud to be in the fold.

9. Good luck. This hard work is definitely worth the effort. As Walt Disney said, "It's fun to do the impossible...there is less competition."

EXERCISE

1. What does "dynasty" mean to you?

_____

_____

_____

2. Who can you identify within your family's younger generation as being as committed as you are to ensuring the longevity of your dynasty?

_____

_____

_____

3. Which of Abraham Lincoln's leadership strategies will you use to assist in building your dynasty?

_____

_____

_____

_____

_____

Chapter 8

DISTRIBUTING INHERITANCES

"The inheritance of a distinguished and noble name is a proud inheritance to him who lives worthily of it."

— Charles Caleb Colton

I've spent my professional life dealing with the above saying and how to apply it to the lives of those who will listen.

In the area of inheritance and lifetime support of your children, the notion that everything should be equal in terms of financial sharing sounds like a foundational value for senior generations' planning. But wait; being equal isn't practical or feasible. Every family situation is different, as are the individuals who make up the family unit. Better to start the journey of passing on wealth and family objects with a statement of intent by the senior generation that love and caring will be their intent in any sharing going forward.

This intent will be applied during the lives of the family members as well as in their estate planning and deaccessioning.

Take a family that has four children, one of whom has special needs. The financial support and funding for the needs of that one family member clearly differ greatly from those family members not challenged by the same issues.

Then there will be marriages, and possible help for educational funding that differs depending on the schools and their programs, and possible help for family members obtaining their first mortgages, and possible help for a family member starting a new venture.

Start with a clear statement of your and your partners' philosophy of how you are prepared to help each family member live a productive and useful life. Then take each issue on its own, without taking out a spreadsheet for exacting equalization purposes down to the penny. This transparency will help the family stay in harmony.

My father said, "Comparisons are odious." In other words, they stink. And families who stay locked in comparison analysis rather than seeing things from abundance will suffer from disappointments and unnecessary competition and jealousy. So true.

End of life planning, estate planning, and deaccessioning are all part of the art of having family members share in the tangible items in the lives of the parents. Where possible, do this planning while the parents are still alive. Consider hiring a skilled facilitator consultant to lead the session. In the section below, I'll share how we did this in my family.

WHO GETS GRANDMA'S YELLOW PIE PLATE?

When my parents were getting to that time of life when they wanted to move from their home of thirty-plus years to a condo in a retirement community, my family hired a professional to help my five siblings and me approach this emotion-packed process. I had already helped many families over the years go through this process. But I quickly recognized I couldn't be that person for my own family. In preparation for going through one of these distributions of tangible property events, our consultant suggested we all read "Who Gets Grandma's Yellow Pie Plate."[1]

---

1   The full article can be read at: https://www.ag.ndsu.edu/cff/family-and-community-education/who-gets-grandmas-pie-plate

This article asks you to think about what is the "yellow pie plate" in your family? The article states:

> The transfer of non-titled personal property, such as photographs and other family heirlooms, often creates more challenges among family members than the transfer of titled property. This program will allow participants to explore ways to make the processes a bit easier and less stressful to giver and receiver. The program uses "show and tell" along with storytelling to encourage discussion among participants.

In our case, we decided to put all the items to be distributed into different categories: Silver, jewelry, crystal, furniture (my dad and siblings had been involved in making specific pieces of my parents' furniture), china, toys, clothes, and art works.

With the help of our facilitator, we started the process by each picking their three favorite objects and bringing them to the dining room table. After saying a prayer, we were to shut our eyes and identify the one item we cherished the most and place our hand on it. If two people identified the same object, we were both encouraged to tell a story about what made it so special to us. One of my sisters and I picked the same toy sideboard with culinary items, miniature plates, and silverware. The story I shared with my siblings was that in my youth, I had suffered from recurring and serious earaches. When that would happen, my mother would bring this toy to my bed for her and me to play with along with small figures from our big dollhouse. This magical time of "make believe" helped with reducing the pain from my earaches. My sister agreed my memory was more worthy than the one she had in her memory bank.

My siblings and I then moved to how to deal with each category we had identified. Each time we would begin a new category, we would start with the six of us all drawing a playing card from the deck of cards. Whoever drew the highest card got to go first, and so on. By adopting this random lot process, we all felt we were being fair.

KEY POINTS FOR DISTRIBUTING INHERITANCES

1. Encourage senior generations to gift tangible items and property during their lifetimes.

2. Disposing of family sensitive real estate can be very divisive.

3. Use a skilled professional to help family go through the deaccessioning of tangible property.

4. Instill a feeling of abundance and gratitude within the broader family unit. Avoid comparisons.

5. Remember that "fair" doesn't mean exactly "equal." When distributing inheritances, recognize the benefit and the objective, and remain independent and professional.

6. Love is limitless.

EXERCISE

1. Draft a statement for what your family's donor philosophy is. Get feedback from other family members.

_____

_____

_____

_____

_____

2. What is a neutral or important place you might gather for discussing distribution of inheritances?

_____

_____

_____

_____

3. What kinds of activities could you include to make the process meaningful for everyone?

_____

_____

_____

_____

_____

Chapter 9

KNOWING ALL GROWTH IS
PRECEDED BY A PARADIGM SHIFT

*"Almost every significant breakthrough in the field of
scientific endeavor is first a break with tradition,
with old ways of thinking, with old paradigms."*

— Stephen R. Covey

BREAKING THROUGH OLD PARADIGMS

"Paradigm" is a unique word that really makes you think about why
you believe what you believe, yet many folks don't fully understand its
full meaning. Dictionary.com defines it as:

Paradigm (Noun)

1.1. A framework containing the basic assumptions, ways of thinking,
and methodology that are commonly accepted by members of a
scientific community.

1.2. Such a cognitive framework shared by members of any discipline
or group:

- The company's business paradigm needs updating for a new
generation.

2. Informal. a general mental model or framework for anything:

- Their first album completely blew apart my paradigm of what rock music could be.

3. An example serving as a model for others to imitate; a pattern:

- Pelham Dairy's 10-year aged cheddar is the paradigm of cheddars.

4. A typical or representative instance or example:

- His experimentalism and iconoclastic attitude toward the past make Picasso a paradigm of twentieth-century painting.

In lay terms, I believe a paradigm means you experience something in one particular way that you apply to all future ways of thinking. For example, perhaps you were bitten by a dog as a kid, and now you are afraid of dogs, believing they all bite and especially that they bite kids. The truth is a very small percentage of dogs bite people, and usually only when they are threatened. If you hold on to this negative belief (paradigm) about dogs your entire life, you may miss out on the fun and support of having a dog.

Our challenge is often keeping old ways of thinking (paradigms) from interfering with and limiting new ideas about things, whether it be business, parenting, relationships, or money. When you understand your paradigms, you can begin to break these patterns that no longer serve you. But first you need to understand four truths about paradigms.

FOUR TRUTHS ABOUT PARADIGMS

1. We are blind to data that conflicts with our paradigms.

2. We rarely question our paradigms.

3. We see the world as our paradigms have conditioned us to see it, not as it really is.

4. We see major changes in effectiveness are almost always preceded by paradigm shifts.

TAKING A SELF-INVENTORY

From an early age, I had a gift for listening empathetically. I found myself taking on others' issues and feeling I could solve their problems. When I was in my early twenties, I learned I could engage people, listen to their issues, and even volunteer to be their fixer.

The only problem was I was feeling overburdened by taking on all these people's problems, pain, and negative energy. In time, I learned instead of being the "fixer," I should ask the tough questions and empower others to attack their own problems. With that experience, I created my formalized program, which I called "The Toolbox for Designing Your Own Personal Mission Statement." Note that Paige West is the co-creator of this toolbox.

CREATING YOUR OWN PERSONAL MISSION STATEMENT

Finding myself in leadership positions often, I made it a point to study leadership and its best forms. Although many leadership books focus on a leader who leads groups to achieve group goals, I actually believe self-leadership is perhaps the most important aspect of leadership. Once you have inspired yourself to act in pursuit of your dreams, goals, and vision, by law of association, those who follow you will be inspired to do the same.

Mission statements are good tools or road maps for achieving collective goals. Committing to developing a personal mission statement is the key to unlocking the power to develop personal leadership.

Everyone's personal mission statement is unique. For example, I have seen accountants create their mission statements in spreadsheets, whereas artists have created drawings, paintings, or poems.

I credit Stephen Covey's *The 7 Habits of Highly Effective People* for this framework for creating your own personal mission statement.

Phase 1: Imagination

- Initial visualization

- Transport yourself ten years into the future

- What has changed? What has stayed the same?

Phase 2: Hard Work

- Map your missions

- New vision/personal philosophy

- Self-Investing strategy

- Values, goals, principles/truths

- Roles

- Objectives

- Truths

Phase 3: Summary Visualization

Transport yourself to a party after your funeral. What would you like people to remember most about you? What will endure?

These exercises have been part of training seminars for forty years. Many participants have approached me later and said this exercise was the single greatest exercise they have completed. It breaks old paradigms that do not serve them, and they experience massive growth.

The personal mission statement that has guided my life is: To live a principled life full of passion and accomplishment in service to family, community, church, country, the globe, and God.

KEY POINTS FOR KNOWING ALL GROWTH IS PRECEDED BY A PARADIGM SHIFT

1. Unexamined paradigms keep us stuck in old ways of thinking and acting.

2. Identifying our paradigms is key to changing our minds/how we think and moving forward.

3. Outlining your paradigms is often a beneficial form of meditation.

4. Our personal mission statement should reflect who we are and who we want to become, not who we used to be and paradigms that no longer serve us.

5. Stephen Covey's *The 7 Habits for Highly Effective People* is a great resource for generating your personal mission statement.

6. Two anonymous quotes that I feel really drive home the paradigm message:

   "I have learned two people can look at the exact same thing and see something totally different." — Author Unknown

   "Opinion is really the lowest form of human knowledge. It requires no accountability, no understanding. The highest form of knowledge is empathy, for it requires us to suspend our egos and live in another's world." — Bill Bullard

EXERCISE

1. Which of your paradigms still serve you?

_____

_____

_____

_____

_____

2. Which old paradigms no longer serve you?

_____

_____

_____

_____

_____

3. What changes do you need to make to release old paradigms and/or self-limiting beliefs?

_____

_____

_____

_____

_____

4. What do you have to change right now to get on track to achieving your personal and family business goals?

_____

_____

_____

_____

_____

5. What is your personal mission statement?

_____

_____

_____

_____

_____

_____

_____

_____

6. Describe how your future and family business will look once you make these changes and start living every day by your personal mission statement.

_____

_____

_____

_____

_____

Chapter 10
WORKING HARD TO PRODUCE RESULTS

"I am a great believer in luck.
The harder I work, the more of it I seem to have."

— Sam Walton

While the above quote is often attributed to Thomas Jefferson, the record shows Coleman Cox actually said it first. I attribute it to Sam Walton because when he and I had lunch together, he repeatedly used this phrase like a mantra as the foundation for his success with Wal-Mart. So, I am going with Sam Walton even if it isn't technically accurate because he used this phrase, mindset, and ideology as the driving force behind his success.

FATHER'S WORK ETHIC AND INSPIRATION AT ROCK ACRES

My father, James Jungé, learned many valuable lessons about hard work early in life. Born in 1921, my father lost his father, William, when he was eight at the start of the Great Depression. His father, who sold for the Fuller Brush company, died of dysentery. But despite Dad's circumstances, he often told me how much he loved living with his spinster aunties in the small community of Glenview, Illinois.

My dad lived with his aunties because his mother was a portrait artist and had to work in downtown Chicago. She left her three sons with her sisters in Glenview while she sold her art in the city. Some of Dad's fondest childhood memories were of the countless hours he spent in his family's community garden. He hoed, weeded, watered, harvested, and eventually canned crops from the garden that were shared among the community.

When I was twelve, my father decided to share his gardening experience with me in hopes I would learn some of the same lessons about hard work he learned as a kid. What I didn't realize at the time was that he was also preparing me for a number of valuable business lessons. Our garden was to be at our summer home in the Catskills. My father used my summer allowance as a capital investment to prepare the plot and purchase materials for a nine-foot fence to keep deer, raccoons, and skunks out of the soon-to-be garden. As chief laborer, I would keep 100 percent of the profits at the end of the season.

Dad and I set about planning our plot. I can still remember our crop selection: corn, eggplant, squash, cucumber, peppers, lettuce, and tomatoes.

I was anxious to start planting. But first I needed to prepare the ground, which was brown clay filled with a seemingly endless supply of rocks. I toiled for a week, and eventually, I had to enlist the help of a college student to clear the ground. My father, remembering the rich, black Illinois soil of his childhood, thought clearing the plot would take three days at most. I hadn't planted a single seed and already I was feeling the pressure of a shortened growing season.

After the rocky ground created similar delays with installing the fence, I was finally able to plant my crops and started putting in long days in my garden. As the season wore on, I began to see the fruits of my labor and soon had a steady stream of valuable produce to sell. In fact, after a bit of market research, I realized at the Pitcairn family compound in the Catskills that I had a superior product—and a superior sales pitch.

My aunts didn't have gardens, and I knew what the store down the mountain in Kingston charged. Because I had better produce and could deliver right to their doors, I charged a 20 to 25 percent premium over the market in town. It was simple supply and demand. I took a small tablet on which I wrote "Rock Acres" on the top with a column down the left side with "quantity" and the "weights" and each item's "cost" with a total at the bottom so they felt comfortable.

I then went to my aunts and presold my produce with the markup, which was justified by my superior product and delivery service directly to their pantry shelves. I remember buying a scale and installing it in the back of our Jeep. And, of course, my aunts often tipped me in addition to my premium prices, which always made my day.

I quickly learned about branding and packaging. My aunts knew how hard I'd worked to clear the rocks from the garden, and I didn't want them to forget it, so I named my humble plot *Rock Acres* and put a big sign next to the pile of rocks I'd dug up. I bought baskets and green paper to package my produce and polished the fruits and vegetables until they shone like mirrors.

With my core customer base satisfied, I had a very successful summer. I learned valuable lessons about patience and hard work. But it wasn't easy. At the beginning of summer, I was frustrated about giving up my allowance. I pictured my hometown cronies biking to the swim club and 7-Eleven for popsicles and candy with money to burn in their pockets. But when I began to see profits come August, I understood the rewards of delayed gratification and following through on a plan. I learned the value of sales strategies and also the importance of customer service.

When I was getting ready to go home, I remembered thinking about my friends and classmates earlier in the summer, but with a bumper crop to harvest and the proceeds of my efforts, I earned about five times my summer allowance.

Clearly, one lesson I learned that summer was that delayed gratification often leads to substantial rewards. This principle has guided me and my family my whole life. As I got older, I chose to serve my aunts and the rest of the family in a different role. I made a career of helping our family protect and grow its wealth with the Pitcairn Company. The relationships I formed that summer gave me a special rapport with my family, which has served all of us well.

In the following decades, I've often thought of the lessons I learned at Rock Acres. Like my father, I've tried to impart similar lessons to my own children about the rewards that come with patience, hard work, and honoring family.

LEARNING EARLY

When I was eleven, I learned to drive tractors, trucks, and Jeeps with manual transmissions. I practiced driving at my grandmother's old, twenty-five-acre dairy farm and whenever we went to family properties in the Catskills where we had ten miles of private roads. When I was fourteen, I recall massive snowstorms blanketing the roads, particularly the northern suburbs of Philadelphia.

We lived close to a college, and my family employed a number of students to maintain our property. Having built good relationships with these students, I identified two who were hungry for money. I jumped in our four-wheel-drive Jeep Wagoner with a snowplow attached knowing the police would be so busy with the storm that they wouldn't have time to bother a fourteen-year-old without a driver's license trying to do his part by plowing people's driveways. I went into the dorm to recruit these two to sell my plowing services in heavily populated neighborhoods with long driveways.

These two college students would sell the homeowners our plowing service, and I would do the work. They would make the sale and shovel steps and sidewalks, and I would back the Jeep into the driveway and make two swipes, pushing the snow out the end of the driveway and across the road into the snowbank on the other side. Then we repeated the process at the next house.

That winter storm taught me the power of "cash flow"! My father provided the vehicle, fuel, and opportunity, and I suspect he knew what I was up to, but at least he didn't try to stop me. Based on my business experience at Rock Acres, I learned about percentages, delegation, division of labor, and what was fair. Since I had the Jeep, and actually did the plowing, I kept 60 percent of the profits and gave my helpers each 20 percent.

On average, we earned ten dollars per driveway and plowed about twenty-five driveways per day in about three hours, so we totaled $250 per day. My take home each night was $150 and they made $50 each. Back in 1964, earning $150 for three hours of work was great. Doing it as a fourteen-year-old kid with no driver's license was even better, especially when we did it two or three days in a row with every new snowstorm that winter. When all was said and done, I learned about the power of teamwork, delegation, and hard work. By the end of winter, I had earned more than $1,000, Yeah, baby!

GOING TO GREAT PLACES ON FAMILY VACATIONS EVERY SUMMER

When I was thirteen, my parents, uncles, and aunts were planning a summer vacation to Norway and Italy. My dad decided I should be the point person on the logistics of the trip and arranged for me to meet a Norwegian Travel agent who was a family friend affectionately known as "Papa Gusta."

Remember, this was decades before the internet and Google Maps. I knew what my extended family liked to do on a typical vacation day in another country. I got to work with Papa Gusta planning every detail, including things like which bus company and driver we would use. I decided which ferry company we would use to get from our bus to the cog railways and then to the grand hotels where we would stay as we moved from one spectacular fjord to another.

I was responsible for keeping track of the different currencies, tipping customs, advanced check-ins, and how to deal with the manager at each hotel. Traditionally, we would eat at the hotel our first day, then for the following evening, I selected a local restaurant. I had to keep track of food allergies and ensure I knew the travelers' overall needs during the trip.

My father had certainly entrusted me with a challenging responsibility, but I reveled in my family's appreciation of all the arrangements I had made. It was an all-around great experience, and I learned so much about people—it was such a boost of confidence in my own potential.

An especially important lesson for affluent parents is to empower the next generation. In doing so, it is important to have the young person earn income from others beyond their parents. I had all my kids earn money, learn responsibility, and plan logistics, and they all benefited from the experiences.

All my kids had summer jobs when they were in high school. This helped them learn what it was like to work for others, serve clients, and earn their own paychecks. And when their first paycheck came, they all noticed the FICA deductions and had the same reaction, "Who is FICA?" It was an opportunity for them to learn about paying taxes and how and why it happens.

THE RETURN OF THE PACKARD

And now for a fun story that drives home the value of practicing patience and the sweetness of delayed gratification.

After an almost twenty-year trip around the world, "The Sailboat," the Pitcairn family's beloved Packard, finally returned to Glencairn, thanks to a lucky twist of fate. Its journey, as shared below, drives home the value of practicing patience and the sweetness of delayed gratification.

In 1927, my grandfather, Raymond Pitcairn, owned "The Sailboat," the Pitcairn family's beloved Packard. We all loved that car, but for whatever reason, Grandfather sold it in 1956. It then began a long journey before it would finally return home to Glencairn in 2007, thanks to a lucky twist of fate—a round trip of more than sixty years.

My grandfather had purchased the Packard for $4,139 in June of 1927. The bill of sale shows a $500 trade in for a Pierce Arrow. He spent an extra $275 to have the roof raised four inches so he would not have to remove his top hat. At the time, he owned a large block of stock in the Stetson Hat Company, so he always wore hats to promote his investment.

Raymond used the Packard for all kinds of excursions and family events for almost thirty years. Many of us have fond memories of riding in The Sailboat and seeing it used as a stunning prop in the "I like Ike" election campaign in 1952.

Raymond's nephew, Stephen Pitcairn, bought the car in 1956. He spent several years restoring it, and kept it until 1990, when it was sold to a German and shipped to Munich.

Donald Jones of Fond du Lac, Wisconsin, a philanthropist and technology entrepreneur, bought the car in 1997 to use as an international road-racer. He competed in events like the European Motor Rally races and the 'Round-the-World Peking-to-Paris Motor Challenge.

Don and I met while serving together on the James Madison Council of the Library of Congress. Don learned I was the original owner's grandson. When he decided to sell the car, he contacted the Glencairn Museum.

As Raymond's grandson, I worked along with my father and several others to bring the classic car back. We all celebrated this success with a small ceremony and dinner in October of 2007.

The rest is history. The Sailboat came full circle and now is proudly displayed in the barn at the Glencairn Museum. This classic joined the collection of family carriages and sleighs, all fully restored by the Glencairn Foundation.

Again, I share this story to drive home the point that in building multigenerational wealth, patience and delayed gratification are important.

KEY POINTS FOR WORKING HARD TO PRODUCE RESULTS

1. Prepare the next generation by empowering them to earn and learn.

2. Patience, the ability to plan and "plant" seeds for future returns, is always important, but even more so with generational wealth.

3. Learning about hard work and delayed gratification are all part of a young person's development.

4. Providing early opportunities to earn paychecks from outside the nuclear family builds accountability.

5. Earning one's own money early helps build an understanding of finance that transfers well into the adult world.

6. Working for others creates accountability.

7. Teach the next generation how to understand and stay on top of their tax situation.

8. Avoid encouraging *affluenza* (the pursuit of excessive material-ism) with the younger generation. Indulging the next genera-tion is not a good plan.

9. It is fine to identify camps and outward bound experiences for young adults, but make sure that is balanced by having them work for someone other than you during the summers. In my experience, teenagers who work for non-family organizations or individuals are far more likely to enjoy a well-adjusted and productive life.

EXERCISE

1. Which young family members can you identify and support, nour-ish, or encourage in creating their very own rock gardens?

_____

_____

_____

_____

2. Who is ready for more work, opportunities, and/or trip logistics to plan and execute?

_____

_____

_____

_____

3. How can you instill a strong work ethic in your family business employees? Will you add incentives or pay increases for additional work, projects, or achievements? Be creative, jotting down ideas to encourage a strong work ethic within your family.

_____

_____

_____

_____

Chapter 11
SUSTAINING A SUCCESSFUL FAMILY ENTERPRISE

"It is not the critic who counts: not the man who points out how the strong man stumbles or where the doer of deeds could have done better. The credit belongs to the man who is actually in the arena, whose face is marred by dust and sweat and blood, who strives valiantly, who errs and comes up short again and again, because there is no effort without error or shortcoming, but who knows the great enthusiasms, the great devotions, who spends himself in a worthy cause; who, at the best, knows, in the end, the triumph of high achievement, and who, at the worst, if he fails, at least he fails while daring greatly, so that his place shall never be with those cold and timid souls who knew neither victory nor defeat."

— Teddy Roosevelt

Four Rs are necessary for sustaining a successful family enterprise:

- Re-Imagining
- Re-Inventing
- Re-Investing
- Re-Passioning

These four words are part of the environment and culture needed for family transitions. With entrepreneurship being one of the only known antidotes to the shirtsleeves to shirtsleeves in three generations phenomenon, let's talk about how to ensure the 4Rs are all present in family succession planning. They should be tenets of ongoing education and training for all family enterprises.

- Re-Imagining: Encourages next generation family to think about what is possible for their shared future. It inspires creative thinking and energizes educational programs.

- Re-Inventing: By doing archival digs into the family and its businesses over time, families can build an appreciation for the changes and challenges past generations took on to keep the business/enterprise flourishing. Such examination of the past and re-imagining of the future can help remove the unhelpful and limiting idea of "We've always done it that way."

- Re-Investing: When a family business and/or enterprise may be dealing with the third or fourth generation and the normal instinct is to be more conservative and risk adverse, that is the time to reexamine what led to success in the past and see the necessity of prudent risk-taking, capital investment, and sacrifice to achieve better outcomes. It's a good idea to build in some language about re-investing in family governance documents dealing with shareholder returns, dividends, and liquidity options.

- Re-Passioning: Once again, "Nothing of significance was achieved without passion" comes to mind. If your enterprise is important to your family, find a way to renew its passion by promoting leaders with a passion for facing the challenges of the future and inspiring all constituents.

THE GLUE THAT BINDS

In the John Pitcairn clan, we often talk about core beliefs, starting with shared values, practices, and behaviors, including:

- Maintaining our integrity in all we do and stand for.

- Ongoing commitment to entrepreneurial spirit and a willingness to change and evolve.

- Sharing values learned from the Swedenborgian faith. This includes both the doctrine of charity and the commitment to the "Doctrine of Use." No matter what profession you choose, do the best you can, be industrious, and actively contribute to society.

- Celebrating the family, which for us means taking pride in our Scottish roots. Examples include sharing family trees, wearing kilts and scarfs, flying the Pitcairn colors when possible, attending Pitcairn family reunions, and going on family trips full of adventure. We also have family plays, oral history collections, and recognize family as a resource.

- Encouraging family to read John Pitcairn's biography, *The Uncommon Entrepreneur*.

- Employing auxiliary board/family councils, which reinforces the commitment to training and educating the next generation to fill key leadership positions like trustees, board members, employees, or just better informed clients. Employing this governance structure has led to more than sixty family members going through our development process.

- Maintaining various family archives. This shows the Pitcairn Foundation's commitment to preserving and restoring Pitcairn ancestral homes, many of which are now national historic sites. We cherish our carriage, sleigh, and auto collections. We rely on considerable library science to preserve our archives over the generations.

- Employing the best practices of successful public companies. We also recognize the benefits and flexibility that come with being a private enterprise. As we launched the multi-family office as a private, corporate trust company, we benefited greatly by being an owner-operator in the intensely competitive wealth management market.

Pitcairn offers a true partnering opportunity to families and their businesses/enterprises. I always told new prospects, "We've made all the mistakes your family doesn't want to make." When it came time to write a family constitution and defined governance system, a group of twelve volunteers, representing three generations and a balance of women and men, committed to a year of hard work. This was the first time we shared leadership with female Pitcairns. Shortly after adopting this family governance document, Pitcairn women and female independent directors were added to the Pitcairn board.

KEY TRANSITION ISSUES

As Pitcairn transitioned from a storied single-family office to a global multi-family office, we had to make many changes and rethink the way our business evolved. Below is an example of some of the things we did.

Having joined the Pitcairn family office, I was encouraged to sit on the boards of the companies that the Pitcairn company owned. That way we could have a more positive influence than if we were just silent investors. I strongly recommend this kind of exposure to fiduciary boards and their processes be included in training and educational programs for developing future leaders.

Over the years, I have found myself attracted to three committees on these boards. I had served and chaired both nominating committees and compensation committees until more recently when I chaired environmental, social, and corporate governance (ESG) programs, all of which were sustainability initiatives. However, I always felt the nominating committee was the single most important fiduciary duty a board performs. Once again, I can hear the sage words of Peter Davis at The Wharton Family Forum: "Don't be afraid of going after the best people to serve on your board. The worst thing that can happen there is they will say, 'Thank you very much, but it doesn't work for me at this time.'"

MANAGING CHANGE AND TRANSITIONS

We've all heard people hate change. A few years ago, I watched a TED Talk that changed the way I look at change. People actually like thinking about a more positive future; people don't like the uncertainty in the transition between the current state and the new state. Even if change comes with a promotion and increased compensation, it isn't everything and may not offset the anxiety. So, take time to understand their concerns.

I had to learn this the hard way over the years. I believe I am a positive person who embraces the future and its challenges. I believe part of my strength as a leader is my competitive nature and capacity to be resilient. But I've found not everyone has those traits, and I may have been blind to this differing viewpoint at times, which led to completely foreseeable and avoidable problems during transitions. As a leader, it is important to do your homework on how others see the change and its effect on them. Sometimes you have to "slow down so you can go fast."

CHANGING TIMES

In transitioning our single-family office into a shared multi-family office in 1987, it was totally appropriate for the Pitcairn family to go from being family members only to wearing two distinct hats—client and owner. In the initial stages of recruiting new families to join Pitcairn, it was essential that the founding family pay the same fees as clients joining Pitcairn.

It was also vital to have new clients work with the same advisors who served the Pitcairns. We were building a true partnering opportunity for these new families. Even before we opened our doors, we recognized the only way to make a reasonable profit on our platform with its high cost professional staff was to employ first class *information technology* to leverage our high fixed cost structure. Over the years, Pitcairn's spending on IT was always considerably more than our business peers spent. As a business, we constantly looked for strategic ways to use technology capable of growing with our business.

At one point, we made a large capital and human investment in a partnership idea called *Witan*. This was a partnership with the Doug Morris Family Office, Rockefeller and Company, Lombard Odier, the DeVos Family Office, and the Perot Family Office—all of which had the goal of producing the quintessential family office technology platform. At the time, there was no commercially available comprehensive family office technology platform, which I believe is still the case. The Witan project ultimately failed. But at one point, we had 250,000 clients using the platform, and we were close to shrink-wrapping this incredible package when it became a casualty of the dotcom crash and Witan became a failed venture capital investment.

As a principal developer, Pitcairn gained much from the business processes built into the architecture of the Witan IT platform. The fundamental change based on the Witan project was Pitcairn moving to a *data warehouse* structure long before many of our competitors. Making IT a critical part of Pitcairn's strategic planning over the years allowed us to expand our regional office program and then partner with other single family offices—both being important to Pitcairn's future growth initiatives.

When we decided to open our doors to other families, it was important to choose the best public platform. Based on the historic importance of trusts to multigenerational family enterprises as a way of passing wealth to future generations, we launched as a Pennsylvania chartered trust company. All Pitcairn Family Office services could be offered under the trust company umbrella. We were fortunate in that our investment track record was long and impressive, and it was confirmed by the National Association of College and University Business Officers (NACUBO) as the number-one asset manager for the nation's largest public college endowments for twenty years from 1966 to 1986 when we began providing investment-only services to our new clients. This impressive investment performance was the catalyst to additionally providing investment-only services to our new clients.

One more lesson: *If you listen to the market, it will tell you a lot.* Although we had some early success offering investment advice, the investment market was increasingly becoming a commodity market. Many prospect families said although they were interested in partnering with Pitcairn on investments, what was unique and attractive was Pitcairn's ability to take a wholistic approach to wealth management and help families transition from one generation to the next, which Pitcairn had built over generations. It took some time and no little effort to build the capacity, both systems and people, to provide the same services the Pitcairn family had created for itself to these new families.

From 1987 to the early 1990s, we had the opportunity to offer two distinct channels for the public. We organized a separate subsidiary, Pitcairn Investment Management (PIM), to offer institutional investment products in all areas of US equities and investment management channels: brokers, wrap accounts, and mutual funds. The other Pitcairn subsidiary, Pitcairn Trust Company, offered a complete family office platform. Operating both proved to be a good diversification of Pitcairn's approach to the overall market. One appeal of PIM was that we were an owner/operator enterprise offering a sophisticated, broad US equity product group focused on after tax returns. Remember, "It's what you keep that counts."

Products tend to have much higher profit margins than the comprehensive advice business of family office services. However, even though products may do well for long periods, they can be far more volatile.

Another appeal of Pitcairn Trust was offering the same comprehensive services we provided to the Pitcairn family to our new partnering families. Comprehensive services took much longer to sell. With some families, this business model could take up to ten years of prospecting before they signed on.

We learned the hard way that by leading with talking about our team of professionals—accountants, tax specialists, investment specialists, estate planners, corporate attorneys, and insurance administrators—we inevitably posed a threat to all the multigenerational family group's existing service providers. These professionals were super-competitive and found all kinds of ways to throw us under the bus. Because our primary marketing approach was offering to partner with these new families, we had to be seen as collaborating with their existing professional service providers. To do so, we dramatically changed our marketing pitch to highlight stories of partnering with the other professional service providers the family had in place.

One benefit of seamlessly combining our IT platform and systems with Microsoft's SharePoint collaboration platform was it allowed us to authentically demonstrate how this approach could work with these other professionals and our value to our new clients. I was proud of having both channels to attract new business opportunities. But things change. Almost all our prospect families had a family business consultant, and almost all of these consultants asked, "Do you charge additional fees for advising families?" We only charged an additional fee for helping clients with their Investment Policy Statement (IPS). We would provide numerous investment products to satisfy their Investment Allocation for US Equities with PIM Products. To me, it was the only way we could control the tax bite on a client's investments. Pitcairn always wanted to be mindful of taxes. But the potential client's provider would often respond, "Dirk, do you really think from Jenkintown, Pennsylvania (Pitcairn's corporate headquarters), that your small cap growth portfolio investments are the best of breed across all small cap managers?"

This was a difficult hurdle because Pitcairn had to expand from using just its own products if it were to offer consulting services that were impartial. When a wealth advisor uses others' products and not their own proprietary products to manage their clients' wealth, it is called "open architecture." Many of the prospective families potentially interested in partnering with Pitcairn Trust Company were using consultants to help them find the right firm. These consultants were all committed to firms that used open architecture. Therefore, Pitcairn had to change to compete. Using open architecture and determining how to deal with this competitive threat became common themes in our board meetings. The subject was a little more than uncomfortable. We needed to change. But change would involve all members of senior management adopting the change and implementing a major reorganization.

Most importantly, being an optimist, I was positioning the support of the sitting CEO and chief investment officer to adapt and lead us through the change. We had to transition the investment professionals' primary focus from stocks to selecting managers. One of my more difficult decisions as chair, which had the unanimous support of our board, was to boldly adopt "complete open architecture." This transition was implemented with due care, factoring in all aspects affecting our clients, employees, and shareholders and the implications to our strategic institutions. Unfortunately, not all members of senior management supported the change, so they had to be replaced. I had entrusted Leslie Voth with implementing the transition, and upon my recommendation, the board promoted Leslie from her role as Senior Vice President of Client Services to President of Pitcairn Trust Company. I felt gratified by the broad support Pitcairn received from our clients and the overall market for this bold move.

KEY POINTS FOR SUSTAINING A SUCCESSFUL FAMILY ENTERPRISE

1. Be open to change.

2. Ensure change is well thought out.

3. Always be re-imagining, re-inventing, re-investing, and re-passioning (renewing your passion) for the business.

EXERCISE

1. Re-Imagining—what is actually possible for the next generation of your family enterprise?

_____

_____

_____

_____

_____

2. Re-Inventing—who can lead this exercise for the next generation of your family enterprise?

_____

_____

_____

_____

_____

3. Re-Investing—what is an acceptable risk when it will affect the next generation more than the current decision makers? How much capital investment is appropriate?

_____

_____

_____

_____

_____

4. Re-Passioning—where is the passion coming from and who has the fire to make things happen?

_____

_____

_____

_____

_____

Chapter 12
MAKING EFFECTIVE DECISIONS
AND RESOLVING CONFLICT

"Once you make a decision, the universe conspires to make it happen."
— Ralph Waldo Emerson

I found that family enterprises are often the worst at explicitly writing down and sharing the "rules of the game," i.e., communicating how things work to other family members who are not in the business or enterprise. When a younger family member doesn't follow the "rules," older family leaders, when asked why that happened, say, "Well, I thought they would know." How can they know if the rules aren't written and shared?

RULES OF THE GAME AKA FAMILY ENTERPRISE CONSTITUTION AND GOVERNANCE STRUCTURES

"You have to learn the rules of the game.
And then you have to play better than anyone else."
— Albert Einstein

Seeing these issues over and over again, I came up with the "Rules of the Game."

Below, I've listed the major topics that need to be included, defined, and explained in every family enterprise's constitution:

Rule #1: Leadership

Rule #2: Succession

Rule #3: Ownership

Rule #4: Conflict Management

Rule #5: Decision Making

Rule #6: Employment Policies

I recommend using a skilled family business consultant to facilitate the development of your family constitution. The process may start with a family assessment survey such as the FEAT (family enterprise assessment tool) I shared previously.

MAINTAINING A POSITIVE ATTITUDE

> *"Be gentle with you.*
> *Be gentle with all.*
> *"Be the peace!"*
>
> — Sherry Bruckner

Keep a positive attitude at all times, especially during conflict. This is very important. One of my all-time favorite quotes, one that drives this point home, is from evangelical Christian pastor, author, educator, and radio preacher Charles R. Swindoll:

> The longer I live, the more I realize the impact of attitude on life. Attitude to me is more important than facts. It is more important than the past, than education, than money, than circumstances, than failures, than successes, than what other people think or say or do. It is more important than appearance, giftedness, or skill. It will make or break a company…a church…a home. The remarkable thing is you have a choice every day regarding the attitude you will embrace for that day. We cannot change our past…we cannot change the fact that people will act a certain

way. We cannot change the inevitable. The only thing we can do is play on the one string we have and that is our attitude. I am convinced that life is 10 percent what happens to me and 90 percent how I react to it. And so it is with you. We are in charge of our Attitudes.

When dealing with conflict, accusatory words are often used in describing the situation. "They may have a conflict of interest." We need to know that leaving expressions like that unresolved plants the seeds that destroy the trust necessary for successful shared activities and conflict resolution. Take the time to unpack the accusations involved in conflict. It's important to know the distinction between perceived and real or actual conflict.

Often, a "conflict of interest" has legal ramifications. But when an individual has major influence over an organization's decisions but does not benefit, it may actually be a "confluence" of interest, not a "conflict."

FACILITATING CONSENSUS

I am a student of decision-making models and have seen how the manner in which a decision is made is often as important as the decision itself.

It is important to attempt to employ consensus building instead of simply voting and letting the majority rule, which can cause resentment in those opposed to the majority's view. Majority rule produces winners and losers. We should appreciate this reality and work to mitigate its negative effects. I like to see "consensus" wherever possible, only falling back on majority rule as a last resort.

I have developed this equation to highlight key elements of consensus decision making:

$$ED = Q \times A$$

This is where *effective decisions* (ED) include a commitment to the *quality* (Q) of the process, ensuring you take the necessary time, have the relevant information, have a clear view of background information, and everyone is respectfully heard. Then you multiply the quality by the level of *acceptance* (A) experienced throughout the decision-making process.

Often, my view of effective decision making, where ED = Q x A, can be used to address conflicts.

EFFECTIVE DECISION MAKING

> *"It's not hard to make decisions when you know what your values are."*
>
> — Roy Disney

To truly be an effective decision maker, you need to understand what consensus is, what it is not, how to make fair and equitable decisions, and which responsibilities are needed to best implement decisions.

Consensus Is...

- Finding a proposal all members can support; no member opposes it.

Consensus Is Not...

- A unanimous vote—a consensus may not meet everyone's primary priorities.

- A majority vote—with voting, only the majority gets what they are happy with; the minority may not get what they want at all, which is not what consensus is all about.

What Consensus Requires...

- Time

- Active participation by all group members

- Communications skills: listening, conflict resolution, discussion facilitation

- Creative thinking and open-mindedness

Going back to one of my seven elements for sustaining multigenerational family enterprises, I stressed the importance of explicitly committing to writing the rules of the game so that all constituents affected are informed.

One key way to instill trust in a family system is to look at the way they communicate how decisions will affect the family. Corporate governance, in general, is based on majority rule. I have found that families practicing consensus promote improved family culture.

Many examples show that when making decisions, if you do not take the time needed to ensure you have gathered the best information and data, it dramatically decreases stakeholder acceptance.

Practicing consensus (the Quakers were perfect examples of this) requires patience. As chair of any organization, knowing if the process becomes deadlocked that you have the power to switch to majority rule is a helpful failsafe. I learned as chair not to go for a quick vote. I needed to spend more time with the people involved, and in taking time, the results always seemed better.

KEY POINTS FOR MAKING EFFECTIVE DECISIONS AND RESOLVING CONFLICT

1. Maintain a positive attitude.

2. Determine the rules of the game by creating a family constitution. Then communicate those rules to the family.

3. Identify and remove the "seeds of conflict."

4. ED = Q x A: *effective decisions* (ED) equal commitment to high *quality* (Q) multiplied by level of *acceptance* (A).

5. Consensus is not majority rule, nor is it necessarily unanimous. It is what works for everyone, so most, if not all, must compromise.

6. Be patient when imagining, suggesting, championing, and implementing change.

7. Strive for full, active participation.

EXERCISE

1. Describe a time a family business member made a mistake because they didn't know the rules. What was the business result?

_____

_____

_____

2. Other than the rules outlined above, which additional rules will you implement within the family enterprise?

_____

_____

_____

_____

3. Describe your operation's decision-making process.

_____

_____

_____

_____

4. List ways to make decision making more fair and equitable to everyone affected.

_____

_____

_____

_____

5. Identify the changes needed to achieve "active participation" in decision making within your family business.

_____

_____

_____

_____

6. What unresolved seeds of conflict are currently undermining your family business?

_____

_____

_____

_____

7. What legal consequences could these unresolved conflicts cause down the road if not resolved?

_____

_____

_____

_____

8. What can you do now to resolve these conflicts to prevent possible catastrophic results later?

_____

_____

_____

_____

9. Practicing consensus takes time and practice but can fundamentally raise constituent trust. Review your "Family Enterprises Decision-Making Process" and describe how you can improve and update it.

_____

_____

_____

_____

Dirk with Grandmother
Mildred Glenn Pitcairn circa 1950

Dirk with Mother Bethel Pitcairn Jungé
circa 1950

Parents' wedding, Bethel Pitcairn
to Jim Jungé, 1943

Mother's wedding photo,
Bethel Pitcairn Jungé 1943

Grandpa Raymond Pitcairn with model of his home Glencairn, older brother Jan, and Dirk circa 1953

Dirk circa 1953 (left) and 1967 high school yearbook photo (right)

Dirk photobomb, President "Ike" and wife "Mamie" Eisenhower circa 1957

Grandpa Raymond, President Eisenhower, and Uncle Lachlan Pitcairn camo for crow hunting

Grandparents with President Ike and Mamie Eisenhower in Glencairn

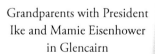

Dirk with bust of President of Eisenhower,
Greenbrier, West Virginia

Wedding of Dirk Jungé to
Judith Abele, June 18, 1971

Judy Abele high school yearbook
photo, 1965

Dirk & Judy in Grand Cayman
circa 1990

Dirk & Judy circa 2013

Dirk Jungé Clan at Scottish Fest, Edinburgh, Scotland, 2000

Dirk Jungé Family on tower at Tonche Mountain circa 1985

Dirk Jungé Family, Tonche Mountain, circa 2007

Dirk Jungé 2nd generation, Sagamore Hotel, Lake George, NY, circa 1999

Dirk and daughters, Jamaica, circa 2020

Three Jungé Generations, circa 2017

Drone Aerial of Cathedral and surrounding Bryn Athyn, 2018

Aerial of Bryn Athyn
Historic District, 2013

Aerial of Bryn Athyn Cathedral, 2019

Plaque recognizing Bryn Athyn
Historic District

Bryn Athyn Cathedral (left) and
its inspiration for Phillip Johnson's
designed Corporate Headquarters 1
PPG Place (right)

Corporate Headquarters
1 PPG Place

Pittsburgh skyline
circa 2021

Pitcairn autogyros
over Battery Park
NYC circa 1929

Dirk flying ultralight past tower at
Tonche Mountain with Ashokan
Water Reservoir in background

One of the Helicopter Service
helicopters decaled for film *Up Close and
Personal* with actress Michelle Pfeiffer

N12J in flight

Dirk with N12J

Helicopter Services Jacket

Dirk with Super Cub after
near-death experience

Dirk on Harley
Davidson Ultra-Glide
4 Corners circa 2016

Clay Riddell, Jim Jungé, and Dirk Jungé

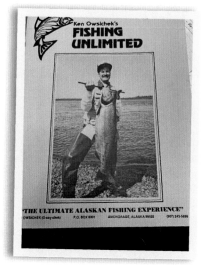

Dirk Fishing Unlimited Alaska with
King Salmon circa 1982

Dirk with Sturgis gear, 2018

Dirk Chamonix-Mont-Blanc Paraglider
Backpack, ready for flight, 2016

Dirk with Rainbow Trout, Mulchatna
River Alaska, 2016

"Let the iguana play through."
Dirk, Grand Cayman, 2013

Dirk diving at "Tarpon Alley"
North Sound, Grand Cayman 2016

Dirk diving at Seven Mile Beach,
Grand Cayman, 2016

Dirk "7 years of good luck stingray kiss," Stingray City, Grand Cayman, 2018

Stein Eriksen & Dirk, Deer Valley, Utah. Stein taught Dirk how to ski "the deep and steep"

Dirk, Grand Cayman, 2012

Dirk and siblings,
Tonche Mountain circa 2016

Tower at Tonche Mountain built in
1929, photo 2022

Dirk sponsoring Scottish Wounded
Warrior Fundraiser, NYC, 2013

Dirk in "Man Cave" at Bryn Athyn
with La Palina Cigars, 2019

Portrait of Great-Grandfather,
John Pitcairn, Jr.

Portrait of Grandfather,
Raymond Pitcairn

Portrait of Father, James F. Jungé

Portrait of Feodore Pitcairn,
Dirk's mother's first cousin

Dirk, corporate headshot circa 2013

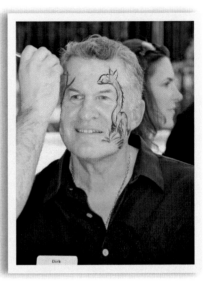

Dirk, "always the life of the party," face painting Pitcairn celebration at the Philadelphia Zoo circa 2012

Dirk's Family Values Tree

Dirk with photograph of Glencairn

Dirk after "kissing a tree,"
Deer Valley, 2013

Jim and Dirk Jungé "loving life," Coral
Beach Village, Utila, Honduras, 2016

Dirk at Iowa State Fair with
Mary Wilson's guitar

Dirk photobomb, Mary & Ann
Wilson of Heart, 2016

Dirk's Clan at Fishing Unlimited,
Port Alsworth, Alaska, Mount Tanalian
in background, 2016

Dirk, Eagles Game, 2019

Dirk with cousin Elizabeth
Pitcairn, concertmaster violinist,
and curator of the famous
"Red Violin" in front of restored
Pitcairn Mail Wing, 2020

SOME PEOPLE MAKE YOUR
DAY BETTER,
AND SOME PEOPLE MAKE YOUR
Life BETTER.

Words to live by...

Dirk exercising with
best friend Moose, 2019

Dirk at PPG Paint Arena,
Pittsburgh, PA, 2019

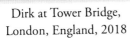

Dirk at Tower Bridge,
London, England, 2018

A gift from Dirk's grandchildren

Reflecting with appropriately named
Irish whisky after writing first book

General Ronald K. Nelson - Dirk's
high school wrestling and football
coach, geometry teacher, mentor,
and good friend

With siblings and parents,
Atlantis, Bahamas, 2016

Dirk with high school classmates and
fellow bikers, 2020

Dirk on a "paint" Nashville, TN, 2014

Dirk hunting quail at Millpond
Plantation, Thomasville, GA, 2014

Glencairn: A Story of a Home,
First Edition

Return of 1928 Packard at Pitcairn Aviation
hangar, Oshkosh, WI, 2013

Plaque on Dirk's retirement from
Freeman & Company Board, 2020

Cover of *Private Wealth Magazine*,
2016, featuring Executive Team Leslie
Voth, Rick Pitcairn, and Dirk

Dirk receiving Lifetime Achievement Award from
Family Wealth Report in 2016

Dirk receiving Founders Award at annual conference for FOX, Andrew Pitcairn, Sarah Hamilton, Dirk, Leslie Voth, 2014

Moose with day-old fawn, 2021

Dirk's Clan at Wild Dunes, 2022

PART III:

BUILDING LEADERSHIP AND INFLUENCE

*"A true leader has the confidence to stand alone,
the courage to make tough decisions, and the compassion to listen
to the needs of others. He does not set out to be a leader, but becomes one by
the equality of his actions and the integrity of his intent."*

— General Douglas MacArthur

Chapter 13

LEARNING THE POWER OF
PASSIONATE LEADERSHIP

"The key to successful leadership is influence, not authority."
— Ken Blanchard

Nothing noteworthy was ever achieved without enthusiasm or passion. I choose passion! I think passion is a higher order of enthusiasm.

BEING A CONTINUOUS AND PASSIONATE LEARNER

I have struggled with ADD (attention deficit disorder) all my life, but today, I believe it is essential to who I am. My kids jokingly say I should be on Ritalin, but I don't share that opinion. I have been blessed with an unusually high level of energy. I have a need to be in constant motion. I am an experience junkie, and some would call me a thrill seeker. If you look at the types of activities I engage in, that is probably accurate. I love new things and new challenges.

I was a good, but not a great athlete. I always worked hard in athletics and ended up captaining my high school football, wrestling, and baseball teams. In my opinion, athletics are the closest things to the skills you need to lead a productive, joyful, and integrated life. I feel that when school is done, athletics and extracurricular activities are what are most relevant to real-life experiences.

I can always tell when I meet someone whether they also have that same experience with sports. I have always thrived with competition and responsibility. I knew early in my high school years that I wanted to attend Lehigh University, but I also recognized that my SAT scores were only marginally good enough for admission. That meant I needed to be serious about my grades and my class ranking, and to stay focused on my extracurricular involvement while in high school.

ACTIONS HAVE CONSEQUENCES

In my senior year, I was on the student government for ANC (The Academy of the New Church) as a social representative for the entire high school. I can say we had spectacular social lives that year.

In 1967, my senior year at ANC, I held office on the student council as the school's social representative. Having played baseball in the spring season my freshman, sophomore, and junior years, that year I crossed over to play tennis. We were blessed with some strong tennis players. I played second singles. Halfway through our season, when we were undefeated, the principal of the boys schools organized a leadership weekend at the Jersey Shore with the sitting student council and the newly elected student council members for the coming year. The gathering included sixteen student leaders, three chaperone teachers, and the principal.

On Saturday night, we had a clambake complete with lobster, local corn, Caesar salad, garlic bread, sodas, and two cases of Heineken Beer. Since we were out of state and New Jersey's rules allowed parents or their local representatives to serve under-aged children, the adults on the trip intended for us to have one or two beers that evening. It was a fantastic meal and a great evening.

The following Monday morning, during announcements after chapel, General Ronald Nelson, our athletic director, said he would like to see the following individuals in his office during recess. The individuals summoned were all Student Council members who were on sports teams and had been at the Jersey Shore leadership weekend.

General Nelson asked me straight out "Did you drink while you were at the Jersey Shore?" I said "yes" but explained we were out of state and our chaperones, including the principal, had bought the beer and made it available to us. He replied, "Dirk, I am disappointed in you. You know well that while on a sports team, you are on training rules that prohibit drinking and smoking. You have just forfeited your position on the tennis team!" I was devastated since I was an eleven-sport letter winner and going for my twelfth varsity letter as one of the elite few in The Academy of the New Church's history. This consequence stuck with me for years and would serve me well over time.

At Lehigh, I entered with a low SAT score, but I was pleased to graduate four years later with honors in economics and finance.

I was a reasonably good tennis player and found a way to use that skill to improve my collegiate experience. Dr. Eli Schwartz and Dr. Richard Aronson were my economics and finance teachers, and when I became a tennis partner to each of these gentlemen, I enhanced my learning outside the classroom just by hanging out with them.

After graduating from Lehigh and interning with the investment department at Pitcairn, I was fairly certain I would choose a career in investments. I went on to achieve the advanced certification for investment professionals as a Chartered Financial Analyst (CFA).

For several years after graduating from Lehigh, I worked for Provident National Bank. Later, in the summer of 1975, I was hired by Pitcairn.

EVOLVING AND GROWING IN YOUR CAREER

On my third day of employment at Pitcairn, the company had its board meeting with its thirteen board members. Tom McHugh, our chief investment officer and the person who hired me, asked me to join the board meeting for his official announcement of me joining his staff. After my father, who was chairman at that time, called the meeting to order, the minutes from the previous meeting were approved. Then Tom McHugh raised his hand to say he had an important announcement.

After describing my credentials and experience, including my internships for him during high school and college, he said it was now time to bring Dirk Jungé into the investment department. Upon hearing Tom's announcement, one of my uncles, a principal trustee for the family and a member of the board, said he had an issue with my employment because of an incident where I had broken his trust.

Because this situation was extremely uncomfortable for me, I recused myself immediately from the meeting. After fifteen minutes of sitting in the lobby (which felt like two hours), Tom McHugh encouraged me to come back in. He said, "Your uncle told a story about you stealing his fishing pliers one summer at Lake Kenozia in Ulster County, New York [in the Catskill Mountains]."

Vividly recalling the incident, I explained to the board members that I had been sixteen that summer and part of my summer job had been maintaining the Raymond Pitcairn family's boats and boathouse. I began to recount the story by apologizing to my uncle for this unfortunate incident, but I explained that what had really happened was different from his perspective.

Every Saturday morning, a sailboat regatta was held. On Friday afternoon, knowing all the boats needed to be in fine working order, I inspected my uncle's sunfish and found that the cotter pin used to secure the tiller was missing. Failing to find a replacement cotter pin before the regatta, I went to my parents' locker, where I knew my father's toolkit contained various nails that could be temporarily fashioned to serve as a replacement for the missing cotter pin, but I would need pliers to hold it together. Unfortunately, Dad's toolbox did not have the pliers needed to perform this procedure, but I was pretty sure my uncle's fishing boat, in the slip next to his sailboat, would have a pair of pliers in the tacklebox under the middle seat.

And sure enough, when I opened the tacklebox, I saw a pair of needle-nose pliers that would work perfectly, so I borrowed them to perform the task.

Having fixed the tiller with a homemade nail that served as a cotter pin, I went off to my duty of scrubbing all the boats. My cleaning supplies were in my father's locker. And by mistake, since I was already on to my next job of scrubbing all the boats, my uncle's pliers got placed on the second shelf of my dad's locker while I was picking up the cleaning supplies.

Early the next morning, my uncle went for a fishing outing prior to the regatta. He caught a large bass, and needle-nose pliers were required to remove the hook. To his dismay, he couldn't find his pliers in his tacklebox. On my arrival to help set up the regatta, he yelled, "Who stole my pliers?" I quickly realized I might have left them in my dad's locker. I quickly retrieved his pliers and handed them to him. I apologized to him and explained that I had fixed the tiller of his other boat and forgot to replace them in his tacklebox. He was mad as he could be.

After recounting my story at the board meeting, and once again apologizing to my uncle, Tom McHugh stood up and said, "Dirk has never demonstrated a lack of integrity in all my dealings with him. I would like the ratification of my decision to hire him by the board." The board voted unanimously to approve my employment at Pitcairn, including my uncle who had raised this issue.

I could have held a grudge against my uncle for recounting this incident from ten years earlier. But I decided I would do everything I could to regain his trust. As a result, he was the first trustee to ask me to join him as a next generation trustee on a substantial number of his trusts, and he took me on many hunting trips and to numerous wonderful concerts. He became my biggest supporter and cheerleader in all my subsequent leadership positions.

This incident reminds me of one of my Dirkism quotes: "The best part of a family enterprise is the family. And the most challenging and worst part of a family enterprise is the family!" I am a life-long student of leadership—I believe the ten keys to leadership are essential.

PASSIONATE LEADERSHIP

To me "passionate" leadership is leading from your heart, soul, intuition, and positive attitude. Passion is contagious. People will want to follow a leader who has passion and compassion, so never feel you need to hide these attributes.

Some of my favorite thoughts about leadership are in these anonymous quotes:

"I have learned that our background and circumstances may have influenced who we are, but we are responsible for who we become."

"I have learned that I still have a lot to learn."

"I have learned that it takes years to build trust and only seconds to destroy it."

"I have learned you can keep going long after you think you can't."

KEY POINTS FOR LEARNING THE POWER OF PASSIONATE SELF-LEADERSHIP

1. Tell the truth.

2. Admit mistakes.

3. Admit to needing help when you don't know.

4. Keep promises.

5. Share credit.

6. Listen attentively.

7. Demonstrate you can be a good follower.

8. Have respect for others and yourself.

9. Be a highly principled person.

10. Be both forward looking and inspiring.

EXERCISE

1. Who was your most passionate leader? What was it about their leadership style that left such a lasting impression?

_____

_____

_____

_____

_____

_____

2. Which of the ten leadership keys above do you need to work on adding to your management style?

_____

_____

_____

_____

_____

_____

_____

_____

_____

_____

_____

_____

3. Other than your children and spouse, which activities and places are you most passionate about?

_____

_____

_____

_____

_____

_____

_____

4. Growing up in a family business has some unique challenges. What are some of the challenges you experienced growing up in your family's business?

_____

_____

_____

_____

_____

_____

5. Which of your actions produced negative consequences? What helpful lessons have you learned from making mistakes?

_____

_____

_____

_____

_____

Chapter 14

REINVENTING YOURSELF
AND FINDING LIKE-MINDED PARTNERS

"A leader's lasting value is measured by succession."

— John Maxwell

ENTERTAINING AND REJECTING SUITORS

Over the years, I became known as "Teflon Dirk" for rejecting many potential Pitcairn suitors looking to merge with or acquire us.

A few years after Pitcairn became a private trust company in 1987, we were approached by a European money center bank to consider a partnership. At the time, they were a major player in stock clearing and other custody work. At that point, their global banking enterprise had few private US clients. They expressed interest in becoming a minority partner in Pitcairn, and we were looking at cobranding Pitcairn with them as they tried to break into the global family office market.

Much due diligence was needed to ensure this potential partnership was good for Pitcairn. On the surface, it looked like an attractive partnership where Pitcairn would immediately gain offices, people, and experience on a global scale to leverage our considerable knowledge about providing first-class family office services. They were serious about making a major capital investment in this new platform, and Pitcairn would retain a majority ownership in Pitcairn Trust Company.

We spent several months vetting this potential partnership. We really liked the people heading up the private bank, a division of the global bank, that would be committing to the partnership. With a detailed LOI (Letter of Intent) drafted, the Pitcairn board tentatively approved the deal. On the night this deal was to be approved by the bank's board, news of Argentina's financial collapse broke, and their CEO squashed all pending global mergers and acquisitions. Although there was some understandable disappointment in losing this partnership, we learned a lot about how to structure a partnership with an institutional investor.

A few years later, having grown Pitcairn Trust Company's business as a multi-family office organically, we were again approached by a global money center bank. This time they were headquartered in the US. They had launched a family office platform but were looking for a partner like Pitcairn that could give them credibility quickly.

With carefully constructed confidentiality agreements signed and in place, we started discussing how this partnership might work. They were particularly attracted to Pitcairn's consultancy approach to the market, selling advice rather than pushing products. With a detailed letter of intent in place, the Pitcairn board was prepared to move forward. We were very disappointed when this bank decided to back away from the deal, saying they believed they could do it themselves. We found this disingenuous and felt we had been used.

On reflection, we ultimately felt good about both partnerships falling through. And we have avoided overtures by institutional interested parties ever since. Sometimes the best deals are the ones you don't make.

This experience with potential institutional partners brings to mind thoughts like:

- If you want it bad, you will probably get it bad.

- Don't fall in love with an inauthentic partnership.

- If it just doesn't fit with our brand—families helping families—just take a pass.

- Good things happen for a reason.

- Even failed efforts have value.

- It's better to be a target than not be a target.

ADOPTING OPEN ARCHITECTURE

As we went to implement this transition to 100 percent open architecture, we were please to find our partner, Parametric, had developed a sophisticated platform for producing positive tax alpha. Tax alpha is the process of minimizing the tax impact of portfolio transactions to a taxable investor. When we had our proprietary US equity investment products, part of the justification for continuing that approach was it was the only way we knew to minimize the tax bite of portfolio shifts. Now, with this new technology, we were able to continue our after-tax focus for our taxable clients.

But to take full advantage of Parametric's program, we needed our product providers to sell us their intellectual property rather than housing our clients' investment portfolios on their trading platforms. Initially, our providers resisted because it was a new model to them. We educated them about how critical this change was since it was how everyone would be working in the future. We would provide audited numbers to confirm our clients' investment within their portfolio processes. Most of our clients were/are taxable, and we believed we could produce between fifty and seventy-five basis points a year in tax benefit by using this approach. In effect, this would offset the money manager fees they would be paying. Pitcairn has actually done better than that over an extended period.

It was a bold move, but moving to open architecture was a key element in our success in growing Pitcairn's multi-family office business.

KEY POINTS FOR REINVENTING YOURSELF AND FINDING LIKE-MINDED PARTNERS

1. Always do what's in your clients' best interests, and your business will thrive. As an organization, it is always easier to fire outside managers than it is to fire yourself.

2. Reject the notion "We've always done it this way." Run to what's new.

3. Major transitions take more time than you can anticipate. If the transition changes your team, so be it. Some may need to move on. If this is the case, be fair and classy about their departure.

4. Look for new technology that can help you transition (Parametric).

5. Look for ways to promote emerging leaders. Your number one job as CEO is to prepare the organization for your successor. Leslie Voth was my partner in the implementation of our move to 100 percent open architecture. And when I retired, Leslie was my successor.

6. Don't even entertain a merger if you don't align culturally. No amount of capital will compensate for a cultural mismatch. Remember that culture and values eat strategy for breakfast!

EXERCISE

1. What examples of "We've always done it this way" have you been hanging onto that you may need to change?

_____

_____

_____

_____

_____

2. What is an example of a merger you're aware of that went wrong? What was bad about the end result and what would you avoid in the same situation?

_____

_____

_____

_____

_____

3. When have you been resistant to new technology in the past? How do you feel about that technology today? Are you glad you made the change or wish you did?

_____

_____

_____

_____

_____

Chapter 15
SUCCESSION PLANNING IS NOT AN EVENT BUT A CONTINUOUS PROCESS

"Diversification may preserve wealth,
but concentration builds wealth."

— Warren Buffett

For parents, there is no greater imperative or joy than creating a better life for your children. For families who have generated considerable wealth through family businesses and investing, this objective comes with unique opportunities and challenges. Wealth creators have the chance to sustain not just family wealth, but also pass on the values and education future generations need to find success and satisfaction in their pursuits. Wealth is an amplifier of all things. If not properly cultivated, the very resources intended to perpetuate a family's legacy can be its undoing.

As Tom McCullough and Keith Whitaker so articulately detail in their book *Wealth of Wisdom*, succession planning encompasses far more than simply transitioning assets. It requires constant tending, including clear communication, good governance, effective education, and shared values. Succession planning is not about providing the next generation with financial independence; it's just about providing them with the tools to be productive members of society.

When I had children of my own, my perspective on family changed. Over time, my father had put me on the path toward a life fueled by the values that drove his success and sustained our family for generations. Those hard-earned values, including work ethic, patience, and business fundamentals, have been invaluable in my work helping our family protect and grow its wealth. For more than forty years, the Pitcairn Company has given me a front row seat to how wealth influences families, both my own family and those we serve.

The lessons and insights given in *Wealth of Wisdom* will provide your family with the key questions you should ask to help your children prepare for the future. McCullough and Whitaker, besides drawing from their distinguished careers, have brought together an impressive group of voices to share their knowledge. They included curated best practices and new ideas from the leading thinkers and advisors in the family wealth field. Their observations and practical advice on family transitions and succession planning are a concise and powerful resource for families.

McCullough and Whitaker are the perfect guides to synthesize all this knowledge. Their perspectives and approaches elevate this book into something greater—a master class in sustaining family wealth backed by decades of experience and generations of insight.

While reading *Wealth of Wisdom*, I found myself highlighting entire passages and flagging pages to revisit with colleagues and family. I found countless takeaways I am eager to share and put into practice. Many of these insights coalesced around three themes all families can find valuable in an ever-changing world.

One such theme is changing demographics and their effect on family dynamics. Individuals, particularly affluent individuals, are living longer, thus reshaping expectations about lifestyles and legacy. With this longevity, first-generation wealth creators and subsequent generations face new opportunities and obstacles. This reality adds increased pressure on families to foster meaningful conversations about difficult issues all families grapple with. *Wealth of Wisdom* addresses this emerging longevity issue from a variety of meaningful perspectives and offers a roadmap for having those conversations.

Another highly relevant, emerging theme is the shifting role of investments within the family structure. As the primary financial vehicle for many families, it's difficult to overstate the importance of a well-constructed portfolio. But as McCullough, Whitaker, and other experts convincingly illustrate, recent and emerging approaches, such as goals-based investing, are creating a meaningful intersection between family priorities and financial strategy. Investing can be a powerful tool in educating future generations and defining family values, in addition to sustaining financial wealth into the future.

As families celebrate and adapt to longer life expectancies and craft a values-driven investment strategy, the importance of trusted advisors is another clear need, which is also covered in this work. Families need experts to provide information and guidance, but they also need partners to tell them the difficult truths and ask the right questions.

With *Wealth of Wisdom*, McCullough and Whitaker provide those trusted services in abundance. Crucially, they step beyond offering thoughtful insights on the issues facing affluent families. They gathered a select group of family wealth experts who offer practical advice and exercises families can use to define and perpetuate a legacy. Every chapter looks at thoughtful questions, creating a natural process for family leaders to foster conversations about these issues.

Questions fuel families. They're how younger generations learn family traditions; they're how priorities are set and how decisions are made. They're how conflict is identified, and ultimately, resolved. By providing actionable activities and essential questions, *Wealth of Wisdom* takes universal challenges and gives families a personal way to work through them. The result is an interactive framework for advancing family relationships and legacy.

From their introduction, McCullough and Whitaker's lifelong passion for helping families maintain their success and pass those values on to future generations is readily apparent. They have dedicated their careers to supporting families in achieving their goals, and that commitment and experience comes through in every passage. With *Wealth of Wisdom*, McCullough and Whitaker and their cadre of experts offer families the tools and resources to move into the future with clarity, confidence, and control. I am grateful to count Tom McCullough and Keith Whitaker as friends and for sharing their knowledge in helping families sustain their enterprises across generations.

Families reading their book access some of the best thinking and strategies on creating a better life for their heirs and leaving a positive legacy that lasts far into the future.

KEY POINTS FOR SUCCESSION PLANNING IS NOT AN EVENT BUT A CONTINUOUS PROCESS

1.   Determine the key questions to ask your children about their futures.

2.   Read *Wealth of Wisdom* by Tom McCullough and Keith Whitaker.

3.   Find trusted advisors.

EXERCISE

1. Identify the most influential leaders currently in your family business.

_____

_____

_____

_____

_____

2. What additional responsibilities can you give them that would strengthen and diversify your assets?

_____

_____

_____

_____

_____

_____

_____

_____

_____

_____

3. How can you improve family dynamics by being more inclusive in both your leadership team and product offerings?

_____

_____

_____

_____

_____

Chapter 16

USING WEALTH AS AN AMPLIFIER

"Are you here to be part of the solution?
Or are you here to be part of the problem?"

— Anonymous

Being a lifelong student of leadership means you do what you can to build wealth not only for yourself, but for your family, your business, and your community. I have learned it is important to use wealth as an amplifier.

The bottom line is money is neither good nor bad. What matters is what one does with the money, which can be used to create good or do harm. So, in a sense, wealth amplifies who you are as a person. If you are a good person, money gives you the ability to do more good in the world. If you are not well adjusted, your money allows you to support bad habits that can affect you and others.

DEFINITION OF AMPLIFICATION

Per Dictionary.com, amplification is a noun defined as:

1. The act of amplifying or the state of being amplified.

2. The matter or substance used to expand an idea, statement, or the like.

3. Electricity: increase in the strength of current, voltage, or power.

DIRK'S FIVE CHARACTERISTICS OF AMPLIFICATION

1. Makes things louder

2. Intensifies

3. Enhances

4. Makes things bigger

5. Expands effects

THE AMPLIFICATION LEVER AND FULCRUM

Much like a lever, wealth amplifies your actions. Who controls the amplification? Obviously, you do. How do you control it? Based on your values.

Each individual and generation needs to define how wealth will be accessed and applied. Determine the purpose, mission, and goals of your wealth, and in doing so, these decisions will amplify your message and better serve humanity.

Imagine a fulcrum that represents your ability to create wealth. One end is your potential to create positive outcomes with your wealth, and the other end is the potential harm you could do. As you execute your life's missions and goals, your wealth will increase, as will the positives brought about by its application, or if misguided, the unfortunate negative effects.

WEALTH AMPLIFIER

CHARACTERISTICS OF WEALTH AS AN AMPLIFIER

Benefits:

1. Opens career options

2. Provides educational opportunities

3. Powers up your philanthropy

4. Enhances your lifestyle

5. Shares intergenerational wealth

6. Provides travel, multicultural experiences, and opportunities

7. Pays for recreation and hobbies

8. Facilitates pride, legacy, and heritage

9. Enhances happiness, enjoyment, and fulfillment

10. Reduces stress

11. Provides independence

12. Empowers freedom

Challenges:

1. Isolation/Resentment

2. External expectations

3. Lack of respect from others (rich bashing)

4. Abuse in friendship (expectations that the individual with wealth should pay for everything)

5. Lack of initiative and motivation

6. Dependence on wealth

7. Potential addictions/abuse

8. Difficulty of unequal wealth in relationships

9. Fear of losing wealth

10. Potential lack of self-esteem/self-worth

11. Questioning "if worthy of the inherited wealth"

12. Wondering if wealth is a burden based on society's view

Although we've spent time looking at the challenges of wealth, few wealth originators or current beneficiaries who design intricate vehicles for transferring wealth from one generation to another meant to hurt or have wealth be a burden to future generations. Clearly, they didn't take the time to build wealth so it could screw up the next generation's lives.

Another challenge of wealth is when the granters of a trust put so many stipulations and restrictions on the use of the funds that the result is "ruling from the grave."

Many adults are unwilling to talk about wealth with their children because they have seen the negatives play out among those who inherit. But this really means they don't trust the next generation to be able to handle the amplification of life that comes with wealth.

Therefore, I always encourage granters of the trusts to have an open dialogue with the recipients about family values and the origin of the wealth so they have an understanding of where it came from and how to preserve it and pass it on to the next generation.

My challenge to you is to use your wealth as an amplifier for the good of your family, your community, and humanity instead of solely spending it on yourself or using it for negative purposes. If "good" is your focus, it will feed your soul, and you will feel peace and fulfillment.

TEACHING YOUR CHILDREN ABOUT WEALTH

When my children were young, I wanted to teach them the value of money. When I put this plan in place, my twin sons were eight and my daughters were ten and eleven.

I asked them to survey their classmates to find out how much they got for a weekly or monthly allowance and what they had to do to earn it. Almost all their classmates had a list of chores they were expected to do for their allowance.

Let's say my eldest daughter's survey showed $10 a week was the going rate. I said I'd give her $30 for doing a pre-determined list of chores. Then I told her the stipulations behind tripling her peers' allowance. First, we would go to the bank so she could open her own savings account, and then she would make her first deposit of $20. She could spend the other $10 on whatever she wanted, but she needed to keep a diary of what she spent it on.

I used the same approach with my other children. They would not get their allowance until they could tell me what they spent their money on, whether they would do it again, and how much they had in the bank.

Then, once a year, I worked with them to identify an individual or charity that could use a contribution and they would make a donation. Usually, they made anonymous gifts.

I call this my "Spend, Save, and Support of Others" system, which supports good causes and teaches them early to save money, but also teaches them to give it away to worthwhile causes and how to make wiser decisions about their spending. In doing so, they learned first-hand the power of using wealth as an amplifier.

I must confess this approach to learning how to deal with money and finances seemed to work well for two of my children but not so much with the other two. Still, I think all of them appreciated my efforts.

KEY POINTS FOR USING WEALTH AS AN AMPLIFIER

1. Wealth is a benefit when used for good.

2. Teach your children about wealth and how to use it for their and others' benefit.

3. Be aware of the challenges and prejudices that come from having wealth.

4. Plan for the future but do not try to "rule beyond the grave."

EXERCISE

1. What worthwhile causes can you support with your family's wealth?

_____

_____

_____

_____

_____

2. Which of your current spending habits or investments are not creating a better world for future generations?

_____

_____

_____

_____

_____

3. Knowing both the benefits and challenges of wealth, what changes can you make in your family, life, and business to minimize the challenges and enhance the benefits to amplify your family's wealth?

_____

_____

_____

_____

_____

4. How will the points in this chapter affect your charitable intent, lifestyle choices, and ultimately, your estate plans?

_____

_____

_____

_____

_____

PART IV:

DEFINING FAMILY LEGACIES

"Surplus wealth is a sacred trust which its possessor is bound to administer in his lifetime for the good of the community."

— Andrew Carnegie

Chapter 17

UNDERSTANDING THE LOVE, POWER, AND MONEY MODEL

"Proper communication will always be a main ingredient for building family solidarity and permanence."

— Marvin J. Ashton

Over my career, I helped our family enterprise and many other families create and preserve multigenerational wealth. I take my clients through a process to help them understand all the complexities of keeping the family and its enterprise running smoothly. I believe much of this comes down to a commitment to effective communication.

My particular focus has been promoting positive models for multigenerational families of wealth. I hope my observations apply to all families whether it's sharing a family business, managing family wealth, or just staying connected with family over the generations.

I am a strong proponent of introducing young family members to a learning community like what I had at the Wharton Family Forum. From the beginning of that experience, I could see that the issues the Pitcairn family faced and would face in the future were not unique. I initially learned many strategies and processes to help our family become unstuck (that is a technical term) at the Wharton Family Forum. It was also reassuring to realize other families had successfully gone through these same challenges.

I also learned why multigenerational family enterprises are so complex. You can use a Venn diagram to help you understand these family enterprise complexities.

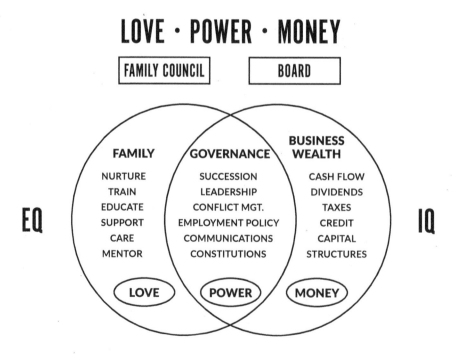

As a fourth-generation family member of the John Pitcairn, Jr. clan, I was often called Bartholomew Cubbins after Dr. Seuss's famous book *The 500 Hats of Bartholomew Cubbins*.

With the knowledge I gained at the Wharton Family Forum, I knew it was essential for me to form alliances with the current leadership as a route to implementing positive change. It was important for me to recognize how many people my life's work would touch. On a familial basis, I am a brother, son, husband, father, grandson, grandfather, uncle, nephew, and cousin. Recognizing the influence I would have in each capacity and the responsibilities I would have to the group was very important. I was blessed to be able to use emotional intelligence lessons in my career to influence employees, owners, fellow directors, trustees, beneficiaries, foundation members, a borough council member, the Academy of the New Church, and finally, in my role as chair of the Pitcairn Company. These experiences have helped the Pitcairn Family Office help more than a hundred multigenerational families.

The Wharton School's Family Forum emphasized the importance of transparency and accountability in family enterprises, and it taught me, when possible, to get independent, objective input. Early on, I was committed to employing the best practices of public companies while recognizing the flexibility and power we had as a private enterprise.

With the above background, the rest of this chapter will discuss what I call the "Love, Power, and Money Model." I have been teaching and using this model for years.

THE FAMILY ENTERPRISE

Imagine the family enterprise is a large tent consisting of both family and a business/wealth. Where family and business/wealth intersect is where the magic happens. I call it the glue that binds or the friction that fractures. The former is the imperative.

To better understand how the family enterprise works, it's helpful to apply the "Rules of the Game" as I explained them earlier. The rules include:

1. Leadership

2. Succession

3. Ownership

4. Conflict Management

5. Decision Making

6. Values and Behaviors

FAMILY

What does the family do for its members? What is its role? The role of family is to:

- Nurture

- Train

- Educate

- Support

- Care For

- Mentor (particularly the next generation)

This family system is based on the concept of "emotional intelligence" or EQ, and when it is done correctly, you create a culture of *love* for all family members.

BUSINESS/WEALTH

What does the business/wealth do for family members, and what is its role? The role and requirement of the business/wealth is to create. It produces and includes:

- Cash Flow

- Dividends

- Taxes

- Credit

- Capital

- Structures (Corporations, Trusts, Partnerships, LLCs, etc.)

This business/wealth system is based on "intellectual intelligence." When you follow this system correctly, you will create a positive structure for growing assets for all constituents.

APPLIED GOVERNANCE

The intersection of the family circle and its business/wealth circle is what I call "Applied Governance." Here is where the magic happens and power lives. The business/wealth circle develops a board of directors to deal with fiduciary demands. Families are encouraged to form family councils to meet the unique needs of the family now and in the future.

Most importantly, you need solid communication within and between both the family and the business/wealth managers so each can work well together in setting up the family enterprise for long-term, multi-generational wealth and success.

When both the family and wealth/business come together harmoniously, it is powerful. It is where the Love, Power, and Money Model comes in. To understand this better, review the Love, Power, and Money diagram below.

TWO SPHERES INTERSECT (POWER)

The intersection of family and its business or wealth includes the "rules of the game."

- Governance

- Succession

- Leadership

- Conflict Management

- Employment Policies

- Communication

- Constitution and Charters

In the Pitcairn family example, somewhere between the third and fourth generations, we could see a clear need to demystify and write down explicit rules for our family system. In the early 1980s, we held a gathering of most of the Pitcairn family. Identifying this gap was the most important thing that came out of that meeting. This was the catalyst for developing a family constitution.

Developing our family constitution took more than ten days of meetings over the course of a year. These were all in person sessions—it was before Zoom, etc. Our committee was charged with developing the family constitution and consisted of family members who volunteered their time (and travel) to accomplishing our goal.

We knew we didn't want to include lawyers working on the first draft of this important document. We did, however, include Jack Robbins, chief council for our family, as scribe, but he understood his role clearly. We did not want to limit our creative work with legalese.

The people who committed to the process included family volunteers representing the trustees, directors, and independent family members. This was the first time I remember the family committing to gender neutrality, which was integral to developing our family mission statement. The governance document defines the leadership positions of chairperson, CEO, and president and defines their roles and duties. It also outlines family member employment policies and shareholder behavior expectations. Importantly, this process benefited from learning the utility of a new governance vehicle called a "Family Council."

Since completion, our constitution has guided us through many challenges in the years that followed.

KEY POINTS FOR UNDERSTANDING THE LOVE, POWER, AND MONEY MODEL

1. Understand the rules of the game.

2. Understand the role of the family for its members.

3. Understand how the family wealth benefits and should benefit the family.

4. Reference the Love, Power, and Money Venn diagram as part of the orientation program for developing leaders in your family. This goes for family members on track to become trustees, board and/or family council members, or foundation board members.

5. Develop a family constitution with feedback from all family members.

6. Avoid legalese and lawyer involvement in the process until the final product is finished.

EXERCISE

1. Does your family understand the concept of having a family enterprise? If not, why not?

   _____

   _____

   _____

   _____

   _____

   _____

2. Does your family have a constitution? If not, why not? What do you
   need to do to create this document within your family?

   _____

   _____

   _____

   _____

   _____

3. Do you have a family council? If not, why not? What did you need
   to do to form this council?

   _____

   _____

   _____

   _____

   _____

   _____

4. What is your family business's succession plan?

   _____

   _____

   _____

   _____

   _____

5. Who are the key players—future leaders learning to take over when you retire?

_____

_____

_____

_____

_____

_____

_____

_____

_____

_____

6. What training or preparations are needed for them to succeed in this transition?

_____

_____

_____

_____

_____

Chapter 18
NURTURING YOUR NETWORKS

"Your network determines the size of your net worth."

— Robert Kiyosaki

As a proud member of the Pitcairn organization, I value my experiences and the people I have met over the years. They have all contributed to my commitment to continual learning and helped me see the power of networks. Below is PPG's slogan followed by its mission statement.

PPG slogan: We protect and beautify the world!

The mission of PPG is:

- We know our greatest strength is our people.

- We protect their well-being, ensuring our employees are safe, healthy, enabled, engaged, and valued for the diverse talents they bring to PPG.

- We encourage employees to make positive impacts in their communities by providing opportunities for volunteering and amplifying their support of causes they care about through programs such as matching gifts, volunteer grants, volunteer time off, and more.

- We trust our people to make decisions in their work that align with our purpose. Whether developing a technology to protect our customers' assets or leading a project to reduce energy consumption at a facility, our purpose guides our actions every day.

- We protect our customers' most valuable assets.

- Our paints, coatings, and specialty materials protect items ranging from airplanes, cars, and trains to bridges, buildings, and consumer electronics.

- We beautify their homes and offices with our paints and stains.

- We partner to create sustainable innovations that drive mutual value, such as advancements in battery coatings for electric vehicles, and versatile, flexible can coatings for infinitely recyclable metal packaging.

- We are committed to driving profitable organic and inorganic growth through our innovation and acquisition pipelines.

- We will maintain our disciplined approach to cash deployment and support our hallmark dividend payment history that includes 122 consecutive years of dividend payments, and 49 consecutive years of dividend increases.

- Technology innovation has been a key to our success since our founding. In 2020, we invested approximately $400 million in R&D in order to create new products to drive profitable growth.

- We bring color and brightness to our neighborhoods through our COLORFUL COMMUNITIES program, which aims to beautify community spaces through the combined power and passion of our employee volunteers, PPG paint products, and charitable contributions.

- We see education as a way to enable possibilities and progress that leads to brighter futures. Through PPG and the PPG Foundation, we provide charitable contributions to educational programs that advance tomorrow's leaders, particularly in science, technology, engineering, and mathematics-related fields.

- We protect shared resources through our commitment to creating innovative, sustainable products that protect and beautify our communities around the world.

THE WHARTON GLOBAL FAMILY ALLIANCE (GFA)

In creating Wharton GFA, we established a unique global institution that allows global families to transcend traditional boundaries of nationality, religion, and geography to collaborate for mutual benefit and the benefit of society as a whole. Wharton GFA highlights how families can change the societies in which they do business via the social wealth their enterprise creates: employment, productivity, competitiveness, and economic and social advancement. The first global family program of its kind, Wharton GFA focuses on research and sharing best practices regarding the social influence of global families worldwide. It achieves a competitive advantage by being the center for global families through offering a wide variety of outreach programs, a robust curriculum, and a vigorous research agenda to a global audience.

Five Things I Learned as a Member of This Forum

1. The importance of an independent director (non-family) on the board.

2. The need to create a family council as a counterpart to the board of directors.

3. The importance of including in-laws (married-ins) by the third generation of business or family wealth to prevent them from becoming the "outlaws."

4. The need for the family to become more democratic and inclusive by the third generation rather than sticking to the previous generation's processes, which are usually autocratic. All constituents need to participate.

5. The importance of being explicit about the rules of engagement. Write out your governance structure and share it broadly.

THE CFA INSTITUTE

This comprehensive certification program is seen as equivalent to a doctorate in investment circles. It broadened my understanding of the many aspects of the investment industry. I was the first CFA (Chartered Financial Analyst) at Pitcairn, which was important to my self-esteem and helped generate the respect I was treated with at the firm.

The CFA program's curriculum includes the following competencies:

1. Macroeconomics

2. Microeconomics

3. Accounting Rules and Regulations (also SEC rules and regulations)

4. Quantitative Techniques (model building and forecasting)

5. Fixed Income Analysis (and portfolio structure)

6. Security Analysis

7. Portfolio Management

The CFA Institute has a complete curriculum for accreditation. When appropriate, investment professionals in your company or family enterprise should be encouraged to pursue their CFA.

THE FAMILY FIRM INSTITUTE (FFI.org)

The Family Firm Institute is a multidisciplinary professional association where all the service providers serving family businesses or family wealth are networked.

Serving on FFI's board, where I was not only a service provider but also a family business owner, allowed me to bring a unique perspective to contribute to FFI's growth. According to its website:

> FFI's mission is to be the most influential global network of thought leaders in the field of family enterprise. We provide research-based learning and relevant tools for advisors and consultants, academics and family enterprise members to drive success.

THE JAMES MADISON COUNCIL FOR THE LIBRARY OF CONGRESS

> James Madison Council: Helping the Library Reshape the Present and Transform the Future
>
> The Library of Congress preserves and provides access to a rich, diverse, and enduring source of knowledge to engage, inspire, and inform the US Congress and the American people. The James Madison Council, comprised of public-minded philanthropists, provides critical support for these efforts. As visionaries, champions, and ambassadors, the Madison Council is truly a crown jewel of the nation's library.
>
> The success of hundreds of projects that members have brought to life since the Council's inception attests to the synergy that results when the knowledge, talent, contacts, and assets of the private sector are merged with the resources of a greater public institution.

Members are encouraged to take advantage of the collections, programs, and exhibitions their support sustains and are afforded a number of unique membership privileges. They are a close-knit community with a personal connection to the Library, its leadership, and its curators, librarians, conservators, and more.

This was John Kluge's vision of bringing together individuals, family foundations, corporations, celebrities, and professionals to raise the funding necessary to digitize the Library of Congress's vast collection.

FAMILY BUSINESS NETWORK

FBN is a global family business network of managers and owners of family businesses.

Founded in 1989 and headquartered in Lausanne, FBN has the mission to offer business families a safe space to learn from, share with, and inspire each other about: how to guide the family involvement in the business; facilitate relationships within the family; and raise awareness and importance of the family business models in society. FBN is a federation of thirty-two member associations spanning sixty-five countries. The global network gathers 4,000 business families—encompassing 17,000 individuals of which 6,400 are next generation.

TEC/VISTAGE

This is a peer-to-peer learning forum for CEO development. It has a world-class website full of resources. I have been a member for thirty years. According to its website:

Vistage is the world's largest CEO coaching and peer advisory organization for small and midsize business leaders. We offer the most effective approach to achieve better results, grow your company faster, and maximize your impact as a leader.

For more than sixty-five years, Vistage has helped CEOs, business owners, and key executives reach new levels of success.

INTERNATIONAL SKYE

International Skye no longer exists, but I want to give credit to its founder, Peter White, who understood the importance of growing and networking the family office community early on. He developed a consultancy including owners and management of leading family officers. This was the first of its kind. For years, the common theme was making educating the next generation a priority. This became the bootcamp known as The Summer Institute, and it is alive and well today. It continues as a peer-led and administered program.

THE HOOVER INSTITUTE

This non-political global think tank is associated with Stanford University. Its mission:

> Seeking to improve the human condition by advancing ideas that promote economic opportunity and prosperity, while securing and safeguarding peace for America and all mankind.

CFF (COLLABORATION FOR FAMILY FLOURISHING)

CFF was founded by Jay Hughes with the idea of pulling together like-minded professionals who were serving family enterprises. It is a vibrant community.

> The mission of Collaboration for Family Flourishing is to bring together families and professional advisors who have an interest in inspiring productive activity on a multigenerational level.

AIRPLANE OWNERS AND PILOTS ASSOC (AOPA)

AOPA is now developing a curriculum to expose students to careers in aviation. With my experience in aviation, I have joined the board of the Aviation Council of Pennsylvania (ACP).

PATHNORTH

PathNorth's motto is to have leaders move from "Success to Significance." The founder of the association, Doug Holladay, was a very successful member of Goldman Sachs, and after a successful career in the brokerage and wealth management industry, he became a public servant and the ambassador to South Africa under the Reagan administration. Later, he formed PathNorth.

WIGMORE

This organization is one more example of the power of strategic partnership. Alexander Scott was a fourth-generation family leader of the famed Provincial Insurance Company in the UK. Scott and I met as FFI members. His family had recently sold their business and was planning a meeting with the adult family members to discuss their future options.

He asked me, "Is there life after a family sells their legacy business?" He knew of Pitcairn's transformation ten years earlier, when we sold PPG, and us launching Pitcairn as a multi-family office.

I was part of the Scotts' historic family meeting. The venue was the Cumberland Lodge, the royal family's hunting lodge in London.

Scott was the primary architect of the sale of the family's insurance business. I shared my personal philosophy about what makes for a lasting partnership and the structures that work for families connecting over the generations:

1. Common value and purpose

2. Focus on multigenerational investing

3. A high degree of trust as the foundation for enduring the transition.

4. A true collaboration where all partners are valued.

Scott and his family, with my help, came together during that meeting and committed to creating a multi-family office platform to be called Sandaire.

Scott and I wanted the meeting to include an exercise that would help the whole family feel included. We asked the family groups to write a murder mystery and perform it on video. The idea created a unique family bonding exercise.

The other part of the weekend focused on determining if the family had a future together as a business. The whole weekend retreat went well. The family decided to launch a multi-family office. The family felt united as they watched the videos after the celebration dinner on Saturday night.

That Sunday morning, my wife Judy and I were shocked by the terrible news that Princess Diana had died tragically in a car crash the night before. The family was gathered for breakfast when they learned of the news. The sadness and grief was such a contrast to the joy the family felt at the closing dinner.

CREATING WIGMORE (A WORLDCLASS NETWORK OF GLOBAL FAMILY OFFICES)

Alexander Scott and I stayed close friends following the Scotts' family meeting. Alex was the primary catalyst to launching Wigmore Associates, a unique network for families and their family offices to voluntarily come together to benefit from sharing best practices with other family enterprises all over the globe.

Based on Pitcairn's and my work at the Family Heritage Investment Strategy, I instantly saw the benefit of Wigmore and its mission. Wigmore remains an important element of Pitcairn's commitment to global perspectives.

Another important participant in the formation of Wigmore Associates was the Myer Family Office in Australia. Professionals and family members from the Myer Family Office developed a long-term relationship with Pitcairn. The Myer family was known as the Bloomingdales of Australia because they had developed a major retail brand around the Myer Emporium, one of Australia's first multi-story department stores. They were also in their fourth generation as a family enterprise and had substantial interest in many businesses and a commitment to philanthropy to enhance the public good by supporting the arts all across Australia.

Another member Wigmore participant was Tom McCulloch, the founder of Northwood Family Office in Canada. McCulloch was also friendly with Alex and Pitcairn through our membership at FFI.

At one point, we considered making Wigmore Associates a for profit in global asset consultancy to compete directly with Cambridge Associates and other global money center banks. We quickly discarded this idea, and importantly, went back to the genesis of the concept, which was to provide family office members a unique resource of likeminded investors so all could benefit from other family offices across global economic regions and thus share their considerable investment knowledge and acumen (intellectual property) with other members.

The initial focus was to harness the chief investment officers to produce white papers and share IP across this community. After years of success, Wigmore membership now includes the CEOs of most major family offices. Wigmore has proven to be an invaluable resource and professional development tool for CIO and CEO leadership of multi-family offices.

IMPROVING NETWORKING STRATEGIES

As you can see, membership in all these associations over the years reflects Pitcairn's commitment to continuous education.

However, with that said, I understand some may be a bit shy, quiet, introverted, and/or not fans of networking. Perhaps even the thought of putting yourself out there and trying to get to know strangers is uncomfortable. So, I put together a list of strategies I encourage you to use to get more comfortable with networking:

- Focus on other people's needs and helping grow their business. When you do this, they naturally reciprocate and help you become more successful.

- Commit to attending networking/association events weekly or monthly, whatever fits your schedule.

- Make it your goal to develop a relationship with two or three other attendees at each meeting; then, most importantly, I encourage you to reach out to them after the meeting and continue the dialogue to enhance the relationship.

- Think of ways to apply your wisdom and experience to the success and agendas of the networking/trade/association so you can gift your experience to the greater cause. You will be amazed by how much your contribution can and will come back to you.

- The combination of joining these networks and joining the boards of these networks will enhance your opportunities to build lasting relationships with other key board members. Networks are one of the best ways to remain open minded.

Your network experiences broaden your knowledge and improve your skills, making you an even better leader for your own organization and valuable to others. This may be the number one reason to be active and network. In my case, whenever I got involved, I was fully committed. Having said that, it is important to say "no" when you should to avoid spreading yourself too thin.

KEY POINTS FOR NURTURING YOUR NETWORKS

1. Look to other family networks for inspiration for your own.

2. Include networks in your leadership development programs.

3. CEOs should be involved in identifying networks that can help develop the leadership skills of senior management teams.

EXERCISE

1. List the active networks/groups/organizations/associations your family business is currently a part of.

_____

_____

_____

_____

_____

2. Now list the ones you absolutely know are a win/win relationship in which you are actively meeting and networking with people who may refer business, add revenue, form relationships, or impart knowledge you can use.

_____

_____

_____

_____

_____

3. Ask yourself if your family business is making an adequate commitment to these networks. If not, why not? And if not, who in your family business can you delegate to expand your commitment? Seeking networks for developing future leaders is a best practice for talent development.

_____

_____

_____

_____

_____

Chapter 19
COMPOUNDING AND
WEALTH MANAGEMENT INVENTORY

"If you don't find a way to make money while you sleep,
you will work until you die."

— Warren Buffett

THE STORY BEHIND THE PITCAIRN FAMILY
HERITAGE FUND™

Knowing where you have been and your successes can help you plan
for the future. In 1986, when we liquidated the Pitcairn Company (the
personal holding company established by John Pitcairn's sons in 1923),
I was among the leaders planning our future as a multi-family office.
As an investment professional, I was curious to see where Pitcairn had
excelled over the many market cycles since its inception, including re-
cessions, wars, and hyperinflation.

When we liquidated, Pitcairn's assets were roughly 45 percent PPG,
30 percent other publicly traded equities, 20 percent private equity
holdings in wholly owned subsidiaries in real estate development, oil
and gas, coal, railroads, leasing companies, and auto dealerships. The
remaining 5 percent was in venture capital. With PPG as the biggest
egg in this holding company's basket, between 1966 and 1986, the ag-
gregate holding company had compounded at a spectacular 15 percent
per annum.

Interestingly, of the eighty publicly held companies, 50 percent (or forty companies) were primarily owned by the founding family, as was the case with Pitcairn and PPG. Those companies also produced 15 percent per annum over twenty years, which is a superior result by anyone's standard. We call this approach to investing The Pitcairn Family Heritage approach. If your returns were 15 percent per year for twenty years and you started with $1, compounding that would produce $28. As you can see, the power of compounding is the eighth wonder of the world. In contrast, if you invested in the S&P 500 for twenty years at 9 percent compounding, $1 would become $7, which is still not bad.

I wanted to test my theory against a larger sample, so I commissioned Dr. Peter Davis, the Wharton Family Forum executive director, and his research students to do an exhaustive study of the 2,000 largest publicly traded companies in the US. We found in 132 of these companies, the founding family still owned more than 20 percent of shares. Interestingly, they also produced a 15 percent return per annum over twenty years. With this research in hand, I felt even I could sell this concept to the market. When Pitcairn opened its doors, I knew this concept would resonate with our client prospects.

Clearly, not all substantially family-owned stocks are good investments. Such was the case with Wang Laboratories. But this strategy allowed me to go into the market with an investment strategy multigenerational families could relate to. Basically, this approach was families investing in families.

Having proven this formula for US equity investing, I was curious to see if it persisted in other markets. Because I did not have the substantial funds needed to commence a research project of this type, I leaned once again on my friend Peter Davis to help me approach the BBC to see if they would be interested in filming a documentary on British companies to determine if the family heritage fund concept proved to be successful in Great Britain. James Reed, a senior member of the management team at the BBC, convinced the BBC to fund a research project with Stoy Hayward, an accounting and consulting firm in the UK. This research also found the family heritage model in the UK equity markets. This led to the BBC producing a documentary on the Pitcairn Family Heritage fund and the story of the Pitcairn's long holding of PPG industries, its work on identifying other investment opportunities in the US, and now the UK story of family controlled, publicly traded companies outperforming the FTSE index.

This documentary was part of a weekly series the BBC produced called *Family Matters*. Obviously, you can't pay for a documentary like this, but it was critical to Pitcairn's early marketing to clients other than Pitcairns.

FAMILY WEALTH MANAGEMENT INVENTORY

Doing a family wealth inventory assessment is a very important part of preserving multigenerational wealth. Back in 1999, the Pitcairn family helped craft a special inventory assessment with Dennis T. Jaffe, Joseph Paul, Sam Lane, Leslie Dashew, and David Bork. These were all professional family business consultants at Aspen Family Business Consulting. The results were so powerful I wanted to include some of this material to challenge and encourage you to do something similar within your family.

Aspen had developed an industry-standard, family business inventory survey, but our family was more a family of shared wealth, so we needed to cocreate this new, more relevant survey for Pitcairn's purposes.

(Key for Responses: 1 – Strongly Disagree, 3 – In Between, 5 - Strongly Agree)

SCALE A: GENERAL FEEDBACK

1. Pitcairn's communication with clients/owners in the following forms is outstanding:		
A. Annual Report	1 2 3 4 5	
B. Pitcairn Newsletter	1 2 3 4 5	
C. Personal Finance Reports	1 2 3 4 5	
D. Client Meetings	1 2 3 4 5	
E. Client Educational Programs	1 2 3 4 5	
2. Your family's financial affairs are confidential:		1 2 3 4 5
3. Your company is sensitive to perceived or actual conflict:		1 2 3 4 5
4. You maintain a balance between running a costs-effective organization and maintaining high quality service:		1 2 3 4 5
5. Your business maintains a strong senior management team:		1 2 3 4 5
6. Your business has responsive and competent staff in your wealth management group:		1 2 3 4 5
7. Your family business maintains family values while remaining competitive:		1 2 3 4 5
8. Your family business prioritizes family interests:		1 2 3 4 5
9. Your family business believes growth benefits the business:		1 2 3 4 5
10. Your family business' voting, training, and inclusion of non-family board members works well:		1 2 3 4 5

The second part of this family assessment is labeled "The Business of Family" and has ten scales:

SCALE 1: INVESTMENT APPROACH AND RETURNS

1. Your family clearly agrees about the investment challenges you will face in the future:	1	2	3	4	5
2. Your family agrees about the approach to wealth management:	1	2	3	4	5
3. Your family has a mission statement that guides its wealth management activities:	1	2	3	4	5
4. Your family has a clear understanding of your assets and values:	1	2	3	4	5
5. Your family's values are in harmony with your investment policies and approach:	1	2	3	4	5
6. Your family knows what is confidential and keeps those confidences:	1	2	3	4	5
7. Your family's investments are diversified, and your returns have grown more predictable and robust:	1	2	3	4	5
8. Your family's income is fairly divided between investment in the future, managers' compensation, and distributions to owners:	1	2	3	4	5
9. Your family has mechanisms to share, discuss, and resolve differences about family investment and wealth management activities:	1	2	3	4	5
10. Your family's policies lead you to take proactive, rather than reactive, measures in the marketplace:	1	2	3	4	5

SCALE 2: FAMILY OFFICE POLICIES AND OPERATION

1. Your family's investment managers share appropriate information accurately and fully with the shareholders and beneficiaries:	1	2	3	4	5
2. Your family hires and retains competent non-family managers and advisors in positions of responsibility:	1	2	3	4	5
3. Your family regularly and fairly evaluates the performance of all your managers and advisors:	1	2	3	4	5
4. Your family manages your investments in a rational and business-like way:	1	2	3	4	5
5. Decisions made by the board investment committee are followed up and implemented:	1	2	3	4	5
6. Your family advisors and staff feel comfortable raising difficult issues with family leaders:	1	2	3	4	5
7. Regular business meetings are held to brief family shareholders and review progress:	1	2	3	4	5
8. Your family has a written investment policy:	1	2	3	4	5
9. Your family advisors work well together and trust each other:	1	2	3	4	5
10. Your family advisors and managers communicate fully and in a timely manner with your family shareholders and beneficiaries:	1	2	3	4	5

SCALE 3: FAMILY GOVERNANCE AND PARTICIPATION

1. Your family council talks freely about feelings concerning family wealth and investment policies:	1	2	3	4	5
2. Your board of directors or trustees are competent and effective at overseeing your investments:	1	2	3	4	5
3. You have clear policies about how many family members assume leadership and management roles:	1	2	3	4	5
4. You have family policies addressing issues of ownership and inheritance by in-laws, including expectations in the event of divorce:	1	2	3	4	5
5. Individual family members understand their responsibilities and roles in relation to the family's wealth management activities:	1	2	3	4	5
6. You have guidelines addressing how family assets are valued, bought, and sold:	1	2	3	4	5
7. You are clear and agree about which decisions are made by the family and which are made by the board or trustees:	1	2	3	4	5
8. You have processes in place to manage the naturally diverging interests of individual family members:	1	2	3	4	5
9. Family leaders listen and respond to family concerns and questions about investment strategy, decisions, and distributions:	1	2	3	4	5
10. You have clearly articulated expectations about individual obligations as citizens and behavior in the community:	1	2	3	4	5

SCALE 4: INDIVIDUAL BENEFITS FROM FAMILY WEALTH

1. Wealth distribution policies are fair to all:	1	2	3	4	5
2. Family perks are appropriate and distributed equally and legally:	1	2	3	4	5
3. You have clear ideas about preparing emerging generations to share power and work as a team with others in their generation:	1	2	3	4	5
4. Your adult family members are emotionally able to handle the responsibilities and challenges of wealth:	1	2	3	4	5
5. Your options as individuals to buy, sell, and make decisions about your family assets are clearly defined:	1	2	3	4	5
6. You have fair and clear policies about shared versus individual participation in investments and business ventures:	1	2	3	4	5
7. You have a written distribution policy:	1	2	3	4	5
8. Family members are encouraged to seek education that will prepare them to make informed decisions and understand the family's investments:	1	2	3	4	5
9. Family conflicts are resolved by the family and do not unduly influence investment decisions or distributions:	1	2	3	4	5
10. The family educates heirs on their responsibilities as stewards and representatives of the family's wealth and values:	1	2	3	4	5

SCALE 5: ESTATE PLANNING, STEWARDSHIP, AND CONTINUITY

1. The estate plan for the older generations is clearly understood by the rest of the family:	1	2	3	4	5
2. Your family exchanges views about philanthropy and community service:	1	2	3	4	5
3. Your immediate family has discussed attitudes about wealth, investment, and inheritance:	1	2	3	4	5
4. As a group, you are investing in the development of the next generation of family stewards:	1	2	3	4	5
5. Your family can maintain the family's asset base, while supporting the financial and lifestyle needs of the older generation:	1	2	3	4	5
6. The next generation of heirs feels plans for the future of family assets are fair:	1	2	3	4	5
7. Your family teaches your children to be responsible in how they manage money and finances:	1	2	3	4	5
8. Your family believes estate plans should be understood by beneficiaries and their guardians as early as possible:	1	2	3	4	5
9. Family leaders are responsive to younger members' requests to consider new ideas and innovation:	1	2	3	4	5
10. You have had discussions about and made plans to pass responsibility for the family's investments to the next generation:	1	2	3	4	5

SCALE 6: TRUST, FAIRNESS, AND FAMILY CONNECTING

1. People in your immediate family trust each other's motives and intentions:	1	2	3	4	5
2. Your family gatherings are in an emotionally safe place:	1	2	3	4	5
3. In your family, you are open and honest with one another:	1	2	3	4	5
4. Past conflicts have been settled without buildup of ongoing resentment or negative feelings:	1	2	3	4	5
5. Love and affection is shown equally to all children and grandchildren:	1	2	3	4	5
6. Your family openly expresses affection for one another:	1	2	3	4	5
7. In-laws are fully accepted and feel like part of the family:	1	2	3	4	5
8. Family members are not jealous of what other family members have:	1	2	3	4	5
9. The younger generation of your family is seen to be acquiring strong values from the older generations:	1	2	3	4	5
10. I trust all my family members in matters of the family's long-term financial interests:	1	2	3	4	5

SCALE 7: QUALITY OF LIFE

1. Family members truly care about each other:	1	2	3	4	5
2. Family members clearly enjoy being with each other:	1	2	3	4	5
3. Alcohol or substance abuse is not a problem in your family:	1	2	3	4	5
4. The family spends time together relaxing in non-business activities:	1	2	3	4	5
5. Your family is active in the community:	1	2	3	4	5
6. Everyone is active in fitness and caring for their health:	1	2	3	4	5
7. Your family has activities where all learn together:	1	2	3	4	5
8. Family members have outside hobbies and interests	1	2	3	4	5
9. Family gatherings are fun and go well:	1	2	3	4	5
10. Family members are involved in charitable activities:	1	2	3	4	5

SCALE 8: COMMUNICATION AND RESOLVING CONFLICT

1. Your family shares dreams and visions for the future with one another:	1	2	3	4	5
2. You have a free and open flow of information in the family:	1	2	3	4	5
3. Your family communicates well with each other about what all family members want from the family assets and the family itself:	1	2	3	4	5
4. Your family is able to resolve major conflicts and differences with one another:	1	2	3	4	5
5. When a family member has a problem with another, they deal with that person directly:	1	2	3	4	5
6. Your family has clear and separate processes for making decisions about ownership, asset management, and family issues:	1	2	3	4	5
7. Your family can communicate openly about sensitive or uncomfortable issues:	1	2	3	4	5
8. Your family is willing to share bad news:	1	2	3	4	5
9. Your family is responsive to one another's concerns and feelings:	1	2	3	4	5
10. Your family listens to each other:	1	2	3	4	5

SCALE 9: BALANCING SELF AND FAMILY INTERESTS

1. Your family shares a sense of purpose that guides your lives:	1	2	3	4	5
2. Family members respect each other's privacy:	1	2	3	4	5
3. Your family is tolerant of differences in beliefs and opinions within the family:	1	2	3	4	5
4. Your family has regular meetings to discuss issues that are important to the family:	1	2	3	4	5
5. Family members do not try to achieve success at another family member's expense:	1	2	3	4	5
6. Your family is highly respected in your community:	1	2	3	4	5
7. The family provides members with adequate material and emotional resources to ensure their future success:	1	2	3	4	5
8. Your family encourages members to be self-reliant:	1	2	3	4	5
9. Your family is as supportive of members who choose careers independent of the family assets as you are to those who work for the family business office:	1	2	3	4	5
10. Your family has produced psychologically healthy and productive people:	1	2	3	4	5

SCALE 10: INDIVIDUAL GROWTH AND DEVELOPMENT

1. Your family gives you credit for your personal accomplishments and milestones:	1 2 3 4 5
2. You are being adequately prepared for your future:	1 2 3 4 5
3. You know what you want your life to be about:	1 2 3 4 5
4. Your family encourages you to develop a sense of purpose separate from the assets the family owns:	1 2 3 4 5
5. Your family encourages you to find your own way:	1 2 3 4 5
6. You have been given due credit for your contributions to the interests of the family:	1 2 3 4 5
7. You feel secure about your future:	1 2 3 4 5
8. You are satisfied with the trust and fairness between you and other family members:	1 2 3 4 5
9. You feel your family understands you:	1 2 3 4 5
10: Your family likes you for who you are:	1 2 3 4 5

This survey addresses both "The Business of Wealth" and "The Business of the Family." I encourage your family to use this survey or FEAT to create meaningful feedback on issues of leadership in your family business, its wealth, and the family.

KEY POINTS FOR COMPOUNDING AND WEALTH MANAGEMENT INVENTORY

1. Compounding and wealth management inventory may appear to be two different subjects. However, you cannot improve that which you don't measure. Or put another way, what you do not measure, you cannot improve.

2. Compound interest is a key metric to building and sustaining multigenerational wealth. Once you have this compounding

principle working for you, it is super-important to do a wealth management inventory to help your family enterprise focus on improving its total wealth.

3. Part of Pitcairn's commitment to services is to share our best practices with the family office industry. The thoughtful development of the wealth management inventory was a key component of our contribution.

EXERCISE

1. Within your family investment portfolio, where have you experienced the best risk-adjusted returns?

_____

_____

_____

2. As a tax-paying family enterprise, where have your best after-tax returns come from?

_____

_____

_____

3. With all the chaos and change in the world's geopolitical environment, what future industries and technologies (such as AI) should your portfolio look to include?

_____

_____

_____

4. Do you still have an operating business as a key asset of your family's long-term commitment? If so, what challenges do you see with it?

_____

_____

_____

_____

Chapter 20

MOVING FROM FAMILY BUSINESS CONFLICT TO FAMILY CONNECTEDNESS

*"Each generation will reap what the
former generation has sown."*

— Proverb

For this chapter, I wish to include an article I previously published in *Family Business Magazine* in August 2007.

FROM FAMILY BUSINESS CONFLICT TO FAMILY CONNECTEDNESS

By Dirk Jungé

Wealth management involves more than just numbers. A critical issue in many affluent families is a conflict that lurks beneath the surface. A family business advisor—who's also a fourth-generation business family member—explains that the key to moving forward is to develop policies and processes for family governance and communication.

Wealth is a great amplifier. It tends to make good things better and bad things worse. It's no surprise that a family's wealth may intensify conflict, but family members may not recognize that these conflicts can simmer beneath the surface for years. A fair amount of damage may have occurred before the family and business leaders even recognize that there's a problem.

Early Warning Signs

Conflict is not always obvious to people on the outside—or even to those on the inside. For instance, in one of our family business client firms (which we'll call the ABC Company), the father and his children (three daughters and one son) seemed to be working together well. They treated each other politely at the office and at family gatherings. But efforts to implement plans for new business ventures and investment decisions kept languishing. None of the principals would overtly disagree with the plans, but they kept finding reasons to delay meeting to discuss them or vote on them. Scratching beneath the surface revealed that each of the siblings harbored resentments about who was in charge of what area and how they were compensated.

It's important to keep your antenna up so you can spot the early warning signs of discord. Tension may first be apparent when family members start to withdraw or tune out from family or business issues. An increasingly active rumor mill is another sign. In still other cases, family members may start to sidestep the normal lines of communication and form alliances and cliques. Family gatherings become awkward and tense. Decisions may languish.

The most common causes of family business discord include jealousy among siblings when one is chosen to succeed the previous generation, lack of clarity in the decision-making process, uneven liquidity needs, and concentration of control over the family's assets in the hands of a few family members. As a family grows and its wealth is distributed among a greater number of heirs, each member's per capita share decreases. Having the right plan in place, and recognizing and addressing potential and actual conflict constructively, will help preserve family wealth for future generations. That has certainly happened among the several hundred descendants of my great-grandfather

John Pitcairn, who co-founded Pittsburgh Plate Glass Company in 1883.

The larger the family, the more challenging it is to keep everyone happy. Various family members have differing views, goals, and needs. For instance, when the Pitcairn family decided to pursue the opportunity to grow its family office—which has managed our own family's wealth across multiple generations—into a business that serves other families, not everyone was on board. Rather than force acceptance of the company's new direction, the board offered an option to those who wanted to pursue a different direction. It created a policy of "free association," which allows family members to liquidate their shares of the business held in their own accounts as well as their interests held by their trusts, while at the same time preserving family relations outside the business.

Managing Existing Conflicts

My personal experience has led me to view conflict as an opportunity. As the chairman and CEO of Pitcairn, I have come to appreciate that if handled in a professional and open way, conflict can create a forum for redesigning lines of communication, enhancing collaboration, creating consensus and reconnecting family members in a productive and meaningful way.

The way that conflicts play out relates directly to the level of trust in an organization. The process of rebuilding trust begins with information flowing both to and from family members, and how that information gets communicated between family members.

The top-down, tight-lipped autocratic style of leadership commonly practiced by family business owners in previous generations no longer works today. Younger generations expect a more participatory, open, power-sharing style of leadership. In companies that do not practice an inclusive system of management, leadership, and communication, a single conflict—sometimes even a small one—is more likely to spin out of control. This, unfortunately, can result in a permanent schism in the family's relationship.

Gathering Information From Family Members

One particularly effective way to solicit valuable information from family members is with a confidential survey, which can help identify areas of family disagreement and consensus. The survey can cover issues surrounding family, business, governance, communication, education, and philanthropy. In the late 1990s, members of the Pitcairn family were asked to participate in a 100-question survey that was customized for the family by the Aspen Family Business Group. We received almost 100 responses.

A survey may make some family members uncomfortable— especially in smaller families, in which survey respondents may fear that their identities will be discovered. But it's important to assure participants that individual answers will remain confidential, and to communicate that, just as in elections, you have no right to complain if you don't cast your ballot.

An outside advisor analyzed the findings of our family's survey to ensure confidentiality and objectivity. The results helped us identify how we could best structure our company's governance and establish an investment policy for the 70 percent of our family's wealth that is held in trust. At a family meeting convened to discuss the survey findings, we created a vision that we could all rally around. We also developed a plan to manage family assets and educate family members about the workings of our financial company and about our family and business history and values.

Pitcairn has used family surveys with many of its client families to help them create a vision of what they want their legacy to be, to develop governance structures, succession plans and investment policies, and to educate future generations. A survey we sent to members of the ABC Company uncovered their gripes but also identified several important areas of alignment. It was important for us to present those positive areas first, so we could defuse some of the anger and resentment and build on their strengths; addressing the disagreements was the final step.

Ultimately, a governance structure was created with a three-year rotating board chair so that each sibling would have a chance to lead. We also set up an investment policy committee and a philanthropy committee to promote leadership positions for these important family responsibilities. Confidentiality is one of the non-negotiables in high-performing family systems.

The Utility of Family Surveys

Confidential family surveys are a particularly effective way to solicit valuable information from family members. They can help identify areas of family misalignment, disagreements, and where there is consensus. The survey can cover issues of family, business, governance, communication, education, and philanthropy. In the late 1990s, members of the Pitcairn family were asked to participate in a 110-question survey customized for our family by the Aspen Family Business Group. We received almost 100 responses, which is a 95 percent response rate.

As our family had evolved from connected holdings in an operating business (PPG Industries) to a family with shared financial wealth, it was important that the Aspen Family Business Group was open to using the unique aspects of our family, as a family of wealth, reflected in this survey. We were fortunate to have our auxiliary board (our family council) in place to work with Aspen Family Business Group to make this survey as relevant as possible.

Managing Future Conflict

The best tools for preventing future conflict are clarity, inclusiveness, education, and the separation of family and business.

1. It is important to clarify roles. How have leaders come to assume their positions? How is leadership rotated among family members, and how are leaders compensated? This information should be written down and shared with all family shareholders and beneficiaries. The goal here is to uncover who wants to be involved directly in the business and on the board, and to determine requirements for such involvement, including education and outside experience. Policies governing hiring, promotions, compensation, and succession should be put in writing. Clarity and full disclosure may limit the potential for future conflicts of interest and misunderstandings.

2. Develop a policy and a process based on inclusiveness. This is especially crucial in addressing the normal cycles of leadership succession. For example, in 1982, the Pitcairn family created an auxiliary board, which includes thirteen family members at any given time. They serve in an advisory capacity to the board of directors, with no legal decision-making power. The auxiliary board, our initial form of family council, has a clear charter to train family members, improve communication, ensure family are well informed clients and shareholders, and develop future family leaders for key governance positions (such as family directors and family trustees).

3. Train family to communicate effectively. Part of that educa-
    tion is training in effective communication, which encour-
    ages using positive "I" statements, avoiding using the accu-
    satory "you," and being specific. It discourages interrupting,
    comparing, mind-reading (speculating about another per-
    son's thoughts or motivations), judging, and advising. Many
    families find it helpful to identify a "family adjudicator." At
    Pitcairn, we call this person the family ombudsman. They
    are the point person to field comments and complaints. The
    family ombudsman should follow a protocol for directing
    these concerns to the appropriate person on the board of
    directors or their family council.

4. Separate family issues from business issues. The lessons from
    scandals such as Enron, WorldCom, and Adelphia and the
    resulting new requirements of the SarbanesOxley Act em-
    phasize the need for professional governance systems. This is
    as important for family offices and closely held family busi-
    nesses as it is for publicly traded companies.

While conflict is never pleasant, it doesn't necessarily spell
doom. The instinct of many to try to avoid conflict is destined
to fail and may possibly exacerbate the negative effects of family
disputes. One way or the other, tensions and controversies that
are swept under the carpet will resurface.

Sooner or later, the demons must be confronted. The process
of identifying the source of conflict and dealing with it openly
and honestly can be a catalyst for helping a family achieve a level
of connectedness and trust they may never have experienced
without the conflict. This has been the case in my own family
and in those of the many families served by Pitcairn's multi-
family office.

KEY POINTS FOR MOVING FROM BUSINESS CONFLICT TO FAMILY CONNECTEDNESS

1. Consider the use of independent family consultants who can employ confidential surveys and a process to deal with identified conflicts or concerns.

2. Clarify all family roles, including leadership, shareholders, beneficiaries.

3. Develop a policy and a process based on inclusiveness.

4. Train family to communicate effectively.

5. Separate family issues from business issues.

EXERCISE

1. What potential conflict warning signs do you see within your organization?

_____

_____

_____

_____

_____

_____

2. What structural leadership or operational changes can you make to address these warning signs head on?

_____

_____

_____

_____

_____

_____

3. What new strategies can you implement within your family business to boost family connectedness?

_____

_____

_____

_____

_____

Chapter 21

LEAVING YOUR LEGACY

"Do all the good you can,
By all the means you can,
In all the ways you can,
In all the places you can,
At all the times you can,
To all the people you can,
As long as ever you can."

— John Wesley

DEFINING LEGACY

In this chapter, I define legacy, based on Dictionary.com definitions, as:

1. A gift of property, especially personal property, as money, by will; a bequest.

2. Anything handed down from the past, as from an ancestor or predecessor.

While a wealthy family may leave the first type of legacy to its successors, any family of any size and financial status has a legacy to leave to its successive members. It is the latter legacy that, ultimately, is the more important, but when the legacy has a financial aspect, it can be of great benefit not only to a family but to anyone the legacy includes as beneficiaries, such as a scholarship fund for students or other charitable forms of legacies.

INVESTING IN YOUR PASSIONS

I have always been interested in photography and film. Even in my youngest days, I was fascinated with these hobbies. See, I was born in the small faith-based community of Bryn Athyn, Pennsylvania, which was twenty nautical miles north of Center City Philadelphia. This community has a strong homeopathic following, and at the time of my birth, it was committed to home births when possible. I was born in my grandparents' home with Dr. Andy, a general practitioner, delivering me. Who would have thought years later that this doctor would play an important part in one of my passions—creating a feature-length movie. As a child, I was quite the videographer, beginning with Super 8 mm video cameras, where editing meant mechanically separating the film on an editing device and splicing it together to achieve the finished product.

Then came Betamax and VHS video cameras where the recording device was held by a shoulder strap while the camera was on your other shoulder. Electronic editing replaced physical cutting and splicing of film and provided a much-improved editing experience. With the advent of high-definition video cameras and Apple's video advancements, the weekend warriors of video land could achieve near broadcast and major film house quality videos.

Throughout my career as a videographer, I became the go-to "wedding videographer," first for my friends' weddings and later their children's weddings, and eventually, our own children's weddings. This was my wedding present for many. I had a knack for capturing candid interviews prior to the big day, engagement parties, wedding rehearsal dinners, and one-on-one interviews with the couple, encouraging them to leave their future spouse a heartfelt message about their feelings and wishes for their upcoming union. This special interview was meant to be seen after their wedding. I had to convince the ministers I could video during the marriage ceremonies in the cathedral without being a distraction since I was the first person allowed to video in the cathedral. Today, video is, of course, commonplace.

Dr. Andy's namesake grandson, Andrew Sullivan, was a few years older than my eldest child. Early on, I knew Andrew as a creative genius. When Andrew was only fourteen, his father died tragically in an accident. Some years later, Andrew's grandfather, our family doctor, asked me during an office visit if I would keep an eye on his grandson. I was aware young Andrew had been accepted to NYU's School for Film.

When Andrew graduated in 1994, I'm sure his mom, a practicing nurse, was not anxious to see Andy pursuing a life as a struggling artist. As it turns out, Andrew was not only gifted in film, but he was also very good with computers. In 1994, Andy launched a website called Image Refinery. Many early commercial websites were simply still photos from a company's hard copy brochures. With Andrew's rich film experience, Image Refinery incorporated video and animation in the websites they built for customers.

Andy was born to be an entrepreneur. His new company became a roaring success and a major provider of interactive web services for Fortune 500 companies. With a number of my nephews being part of Image Refinery's technical and marketing staff, I witnessed firsthand their achievements and the company's ultimate successful sale in 2005.

Sometime in 2016, Andrew approached me with a proposition. "Dirk," he said, "you've had a lifetime of experience with video and film, and you always told me you wanted to make a film. Well, I've just written a screenplay for an independent film, and I want you to partner with me."

"Let me read the script," I replied. "Then let's talk about how I might be able to help." I kept hearing Dr. Andy's words, "Keep an eye out for ways you might help my grandson."

After reading the script, titled *Bokeh*, I was hooked, but until I understood how much time might be involved, I was cautious since being the Pitcairn chair was already a full-time job.

At our first meeting, I had lots of questions. I fully understood this was Andrew's first venture into creating a feature-length film, which, from my perspective as an investment professional, threw up all kinds of red flags about the risks of this opportunity. Andrew was the creative genius behind writing the script, but if I were going to be involved as an investor, I needed to know how he would put together a team to carry out this production and how much it would cost. Andrew said a good friend, Geoffrey Orthwein, would be his primary partner in organizing and making the film. As a major investor, I would help raise the additional funds needed to proceed. Andrew was fully committed to making this film happen one way or another and would be the biggest investor. All good signs, but still a risky venture.

I consulted my old-school rolodex to find contacts I might approach. I also found my Vistage group—a group of fifteen CEOs I met with monthly for professional development and peer-to-peer networking—was a fertile area. We did monthly updates, and I would tell them about my involvement and the film's progress. I was successful in getting two members to join the production on the same terms I had negotiated with Andrew.

Soon, we were getting close to the $600,000 needed to launch the production. Andrew and Geoffrey went to Hollywood where eighty-some talented actors read for them. We were delighted when Andrew and Geoffrey's two favorites, Maika Monroe and Matt O'Leary, were willing to sign on. They were rising stars, and the compelling script, filming in Iceland, and the benefit to their portfolios sold them.

A bokeh is, technically, the visual blurring of the out-of-focus areas of a lens. The film's title used this concept as a metaphor for the blurring of two people's lives as they go on an extended vacation in Iceland to explore whether their relationship is strong enough to consider something more permanent, possibly marriage. On the second morning of their stay in Reykjavik, the couple wake up to discover everyone in the world is missing. They must fight for survival while trying to make sense of what happened and the sudden loss of all of humankind.

Bokeh definitely had a Rod Serling, *Twilight Zone* feel. Most independent films on a tight budget shoot in five locations. We shot in more than thirty throughout Iceland over the course of twenty-eight days. With the script featuring only two people, the third character was the beauty of Iceland. With this film profile, we were perfectly positioned to apply for an Icelandic government grant meant to promote tourism. We were so grateful to receive their maximum grant of $80,000. Since Iceland is the home of *Game of Thrones*, and the TV series was between seasons, we were able to rent their equipment at a very reasonable price.

From his Image Refinery days, Andy had a ready and willing group of technically savvy friends as the talent pool he needed to produce *Bokeh*. Andrew supplemented this group with specialists he found through his new networks. Joe Lindsay was a student who attended the Academy of the New Church with Andrew. Andrew knew Joe's skills as a proficient camera operator, so Joe became a critical part of producing *Bokeh*. Joe took a six-week sabbatical from his job to be the primary camera operator on the set of *Bokeh*. As the Steadicam operator, Joe had to be in excellent physical shape. He did forty-five-minutes of yoga prior to shooting to prepare for shouldering a seventy-pound steady camera for hours at a time.

A focus of production was to use technology wherever possible to reduce costs. An example would be using drones for aerial shots, not expensive helicopters, and because Joe was a skilled Steadicam operator, we were able to produce high-quality transitions without the expense of boom and hi-lift platform rentals. Most films require an operating budget of anywhere from $5 million to $50 million, so we were proud to produce a high quality, full-length film for about $600,000. As an executive producer on this film, I am very proud of what we accomplished, both in quality and for staying within budget.

Although my role was raising the funds for this movie, I wanted a full immersion experience in every aspect of producing the film. Therefore, I was delighted to spend many days on the movie set in Iceland during shooting. I was so happy that Joe Shott, one of my Vistage members, and his son Brian, who had minored in film in college, joined me on this shoot. Brian is now using that experience to produce world-class trout fishing videos as a guide and owner of a trout fishing business in Montana. If you have not yet seen our film, do yourself a favor; get online and view it!

We shot in Iceland because of its beauty and mystery and because we wanted it to appear there were no people left on earth. Also, since Iceland is so far north, in June, it gets twenty-four hours of daylight. We had full light in the middle of the night while everyone was sleeping to give the feel of an apocalyptic world with only our characters remaining. And, because Iceland is on the geothermal grid, everything would remain operational. Also, Iceland is an island with virtually no crime, and people leave their doors and cars unlocked. Our characters would have food, energy, and clothing available. Therefore, our typical camera call was shooting from 5 p.m. until 5 a.m. (with 3 a.m. being the primary shots in the city, while most residents slept). Our limitations became our biggest strengths. We found our best creative ideas came from what we didn't have.

The kindness of the people of Iceland made our film seem much bigger than it was. As we shared the story and goals of the film, other people felt ownership and pitched in with creative ideas. For example, for one scene we were at a horse ranch where we paid $200 to have our lead actor ride a horse after everyone disappeared. The owner of the ranch asked if the scene would be better if he let his fifty-plus horses out of the barn and let them wander around near the lead actor in the scene (because the world was empty). This type of request would normally cost thousands of dollars, but because he offered it as a gift, it made the scene even better and more realistic and didn't cost anything.

On another day, we were filming on the south end of an eight-mile long lake. The nature and beauty were both surreal and pristine. Not a soul was to be seen or heard. Then, all of a sudden, eight jet skis appeared in the shot and screwed up everything. The riders were hooting and hollering, having a grand old time. We just shook our heads, not knowing what to do or how we might ask them to leave. I had $100 bill with me, so I jumped into a truck and drove to the north end of the lake where many more people were partying with a bonfire blazing and drinks flowing. I was actually a bit afraid since this group looked like Hells Angels or something. But I went up to them and told them about our movie's storyline so they could appreciate our need for total silence for this scene we were shooting at the south end of the lake. I offered them $100 and two cases of beer (we kept beer in one of the trucks) if they would stay at the north end of the lake and remain quiet for an hour or two. They were all smiles and gladly accepted. They promised not to ride their jet skis for the next hour or so. I drove back and we shot our scene within that time frame with zero background noise. It was a big success.

My twenty-eight-year-old niece, Brienne Lermitte, was an essential part of the film's production. She negotiated all the contracts, perfected all the licenses, rented transportation and housing, provided catering, and was overall administrator for every aspect of the film. I gained much respect for her through that experience, and we are even closer because of this shared experience.

When the film was complete, I learned all kinds of things about editing, including sound. We worked with a company in Canada, called Footsteps, that could eliminate all competing ambient sound, while at the same time perfectly matching imagery with accurate digital sound all the way down to enhancing our main characters' footsteps. The finished product needed to be an hour and forty-two minutes, which would allow for commercials to fit a two-hour time slot on TV. A few of my favorite scenes were cut to meet this requirement. In total, we shot something like 300 hours of raw video and edited it down to the final feature length of an hour and forty-two minutes. This made a big impression on me, and I have a better appreciation for why film making is so expensive.

This was a Norsk film, which always appealed to German movie watchers, so we needed to have subtitles in the German language to appeal to that market. I was worried subtitles would add a lot of expense to our budget. As it turns out, we found a bilingual editor who did the subtitles for $200 and a bottle of wine.

To appropriately position this film in the market, we needed to raise funds for distribution and marketing. Thankfully, when we went to Kick-Starter with our trailer, we got more than 600 people to help and raised an additional $50,000. We ended up using Screen Media as our distributor, which made *Bokeh* available in ninety-two countries with Netflix as our primary platform.

Andy approached me with what I thought was a novel but authentic approach to sharing returns from the film. As revenues from royalties started coming in, he didn't take one dollar until every other investor had been paid back. We shook hands on this plan. I am pleased to say with my first investment in film, I and all the other investors got more than our original investment back (which is rare in the independent film industry).

THE POWER OF GENEROSITY

Two stories I want to include here are about "The Power of a Benjamin," a reference to Benjamin Franklin's image on the hundred-dollar bill. One story is about a gift, and the second is about how a "Benjamin" got me out of a tight scrap.

The first story involves a Vistage speaker's recommendation near the end of the holiday season. He said, "Put a $100 bill in your wallet and look for opportunities to pass it on to someone who is down on their luck or someone who may be less fortunate than you." At the time, I was CEO and chair of Pitcairn. The weekend before Christmas, I was a keynote speaker at an industry conference in Atlanta. After the conference, I would be flying out of Atlanta's airport on the first flight on Friday morning to return to Philadelphia. Overnight, an ice storm caused flight delays. Instead of departing at 6:30 a.m., we took off from Atlanta at 9:15 a.m., arriving in Philadelphia at 10:30 a.m. This delay made me more than a little anxious because I was supposed to help thank our employees for their efforts during the year and to wish them and their families a very Happy New Year at a company celebratory luncheon.

I was one of the first passengers off the plane. I ran down the concourse to the parking lot and got in my car. I exited the parking garage and got on I-95. Then I felt something thumping and saw my left rear tire only had five pounds of pressure. A flat! *Oh, no,* I thought. I was certainly going to be late to the luncheon. What could I do?

I pulled off at the first exit and ended up in an industrial park. I saw a truck service station at the end of the second block and pulled into the lot. The entire apron of the service station was packed with parked trucks. Only one spot near the main service bay was open. All the lifts had trucks on them.

I ran into the office and was greeted by a service tech. I explained my predicament and that I was supposed to be at a company year-end celebration of our staff. He said it was no problem; they could fix it right away. He called another service tech and told him to get number two bay ready. They pulled an unfinished truck off the lift and pulled my car in to repair the tire. Just as the tech started working, his cell phone rang. It was his wife, who said the school had called because their daughter had just broken her arm in a gym class and was going to the hospital to have it set. I could see his anguish as he told me. I said I was very sorry.

He finished fixing my tire in ten minutes and pulled it out of the bay. I asked what I owed. He said nothing. I protested. He said, "You were desperate. I was able to help. Now get on your way so you won't be late."

As I went to pull out of the lot, I remembered what the Vistage speaker had said, and yes, I did have a Benjamin in my wallet. I pulled it out and called the guy over. I gave him the hundred-dollar bill. He got emotional, saying he was thinking the hospital bills from his daughter's broken arm would keep him from buying her the dollhouse that was all she had wanted for Christmas. He said this kindness made it possible. He said people like me made the world a better place. We both won that day.

I told this story as part of my year-end message to our company without mentioning the amount. I got the gratitude I felt for being able to share some Christmas joy with someone who could use some extra spending money to help make a wish come true for his daughter at Christmas and a heartwarming story to share with our people.

My second generosity story involves a helicopter incident back in the mid-1990s when I owned and operated a charter helicopter company.

Early in my fascination with the history of aviation and early pilot experiences, I had been excited to learn why all hot-air balloon rides end with a ceremonial toast with a chilled bottle of champagne (bubbly). It seems early balloon flights often resulted in crop damage because the balloons' baskets would be dragged across fields while landing. The bubbly was the peace offering pilots offered farmers whose fields they had just abused.

One August day, I decided flying a helicopter out to play golf at the famous Maidstone Club's golf course on the east end of Long Island was far better than making the trip by car since the commute would certainly be four or five hours both ways from Philadelphia. The helicopter would take an hour and twenty-five minutes.

The night before, I called the club to get its GPS coordinates and special landing instructions. Our tee time was scheduled for noon. Wanting time to relax and get in some practice, I planned to leave around 9:30 a.m. This would presumably allow the forecasted fog on the bay and coastline to dissipate before I approached Newark airspace. At 10 a.m., I approached Staten Island from the south, having been cleared by NYC air traffic control to take the visual flight regulations route at an altitude of 500 feet and lower, passing the Statue of Liberty over the sound between LaGuardia and Kennedy.

That morning, as I flew, not only had the fog not dissipated, but I was seeing lightning strikes on my storm scope forty miles ahead. This was not an ideal situation. Using the Long Island coastline for visual reference, I slowed my airspeed to 100 knots. The clouds had lowered, covering the tops of any apartments and condos higher than twelve stories. After thirty minutes in these tough conditions, I was somewhat encouraged to see rays of sunlight shooting through the clouds.

Knowing your options when flying is critical. My options were to continue on my planned route to Maidstone, turn around, or, if necessary, land on the beach and wait for the storm to pass. As I thought the weather would certainly improve by our tee time, I continued to fly up the coast.

Approximately five miles south of my destination of Maidstone Club, my storm scope showed severe weather directly in front of me. I turned inland and spotted a clearing in the clouds. It started raining hard. My helicopter did not have windshield wipers. Flying slowly to find a suitable place to land and let the storm subside, the torrential rain made it hard to see out the windshield. I noticed a freshly plowed field directly below and a farmer's wagon with fresh produce stacked in it. I took my chance and landed right next to the wagon on firm field grass. I felt fortunate to find this safe landing spot in a thunderstorm.

Across the road was a diner and a golf driving range. I shut down my helicopter, grabbed my rain jacket, and bolted across the road and into the diner. I looked like a drowned rat as I proceeded to the far end of the bar and ordered a hot cup of coffee and a Danish.

Less than five minutes later, a large, burley farmer in overalls busted through the front door of the diner and started yelling, "Who the f**k landed that helicopter on my field?" He was absolutely pissed. He said he was going to call the state police and get the pilot fined for an unauthorized landing on private property.

I waved him over. As he approached, he said, "Are you the SOB pilot?"

I remembered the story of how hot air balloon pilots used champagne as a peace offering when they landed in a farmer's field. My version was a Benjamin. I reached out to shake his hand with this gift clearly presented as part of my greeting. His riled complexion immediately changed. When he saw my gesture and heard my continued thanks for providing a safe landing in the storm for a pilot in distress, he sat down next to me and ordered a cup of coffee.

He said, "Do you think when the storm passes, you could take me for a ride over my property? I'd love to have some aerial photos of this property. It's been in my family for four generations."

I did. When the storm cleared, I took him for a short ride over his property, and he was absolutely thrilled! Once again, a Benjamin came in handy.

Lessons Learned: Being able to offer an unexpected gift to someone who could really benefit from it is something to be truly grateful for. It is indeed better to give than to receive—particularly around year-end celebrations. Sometime ready cash will alleviate and deescalate a tense situation. Keep those Benjamins handy.

BEING RECOGNIZED BY YOUR PEERS

Over the years, I have been humbled to be recognized by my peers for my achievements. Receiving awards and recognition is very rewarding, and I feel so honored. Below is a list of some of the awards I have received. I have included the dates I received them.

The Barbara Hollander Award from the Family Firm Institute (2014)

The Barbara Hollander Award was created to honor the late founder and first president of FFI to perpetuate her profound interest in family business and her love of education and learning. The award recipient exemplifies Barbara Hollander's love of education and learning, life-long commitment to social causes, dedication to civic responsibility, belief in the human capacity to change for the better, and belief in giving to others generously.

The Founders Awards from The Family Office Exchange (2014)

Showcasing best-in-class providers in the global private banking, wealth management, and trusted advisor communities, the awards recognize companies, teams, and individuals deemed to have demonstrated innovation and excellence during their careers.

The John Whitehead Award by PathNorth (2014)

PathNorth gives out this award in gratitude to the many individuals who have contributed, bringing their hearts, time, resources, and voices to our unique mission "to broaden the definition of success."

Lifetime Achievement Award by the Family Wealth Report (2016)

I received the Lifetime Achievement Award at the 2016 Family Wealth Report Awards for my leadership and dedication to the family office industry. (See more about this award at the end of this book.) In 2014, Family Office Exchange honored me with the FOX Founders Award, recognizing me as a pioneer in the wealth management industry.

The Private Asset Management Award by *Family Wealth Report* (2016)

This award honors excellence in the wealth management and family office sector across North America. The award recognizes high-quality service and achievement at both the individual and institutional level, as the industry continues to evolve at an accelerating pace, bringing new challenges—and opportunities—along the way.

KEY POINTS FOR LEAVING YOUR LEGACY

1. Leaving a legacy is not about being narcissistic, but rather, about leaving your gifts, love, knowledge, wisdom, and experiences to those you love—your family, friends, and associates—and they all want to have something they can hold and cherish for their lifetime.

2. Never feel bad about sharing your wisdom with the world to benefit future generations. A legacy is all about you, so own that and bless the world with your gifts—the earth will be a better place because you lived, loved, and shared generously!

3. Leaving a legacy can lead to happiness. An anonymous quote states: "I have learned that if you pursue happiness, it will elude you. But if you focus on your family, the needs of others, your work, meeting new people, and doing the very best you can, happiness will find you."

EXERCISE

1. What is your definition of legacy?

_____

_____

_____

_____

2. Write a short obituary for yourself. (If you don't like what it says, what can you change immediately to make your obituary read better?)

_____

_____

_____

_____

_____

_____

_____

_____

_____

_____

3. What lifelong passions do you have within you that have not yet been acted on? For example, for me it was film making. What is it for you? What are you waiting for?

_____

_____

_____

_____

_____

Chapter 22

PRESERVING FAMILY
IN FAMILY BUSINESS

*"We need to remember across generations that there is
as much to learn as there is to teach."*

— Gloria Steinem

For my final chapter, I wish to share another article I previously wrote. This was first published in *Private Wealth Management: The Reference Book for Professionals Advising the Private Client (1996-97)*. At the time, I was CEO and Chair of Pitcairn Trust Company.

PRESERVING FAMILY IN FAMILY BUSINESS

By Dirk Jungé

The Pitcairn legacy stems from John Pitcairn, a Scottish immigrant who co-founded Pittsburgh Plate Glass Company in 1883. Now, as PPG Industries, the business ranks as a Fortune 200 company.

Although many great stories end with the passing of the founder, a few continue to the next generation. The Pitcairn family story is now in its sixth generation, and the family business is in its third stage of evolution. As a fourth-generation Pitcairn family member, I would like to chronicle the tensions and resolutions of maintaining both the family and the family business over six generations.

Family Office Background

By combining assets, our family has maintained the strength and singularity of purpose to take advantage of opportunities, which would have been out of reach for family members as individuals.

In 1923, my grandfather and his two brothers formed a family office to manage their investments and all of the financial affairs of their growing family. Pooling their wealth in a single office gave them the benefit of integrated financial services. This family office eventually evolved into what today is Pitcairn Trust Company.

Changing Needs

Today the Pitcairn clan numbers over 350, with financial requirements that have changed over the intervening decades. At the outset, with more than 90 percent of the family's wealth invested in PPG stock, for the most part the dividend income was sufficient to provide broad financial flexibility through the hard-produced superior returns, the family was growing geometrically while its assets were compounding arithmetically. Estate taxes for each generation further exacerbated this situation. The diversity and liquidity needs of the family in the 1980s were such that we had to adapt our investment vehicles to address them.

Our solution was to liquidate the personal holding company, and as a result, we sold the last block of the family-owned stock by 1986 and obtained powers to set up the Pitcairn Trust Company. Next, we developed a free-association strategy to accommodate family members' desire for independence. This gave family clients the option, in 1986, to choose to keep their assets in the family office or to go elsewhere with their money. We did our best to effect liquidation and voluntary association in a fair and equitable way. But, as you can imagine, this was a stressful time in the company's history with rippling concerns for continuing amicable family relationships.

Shared Values

One of the greatest strengths of our family is that my great-grandfather endowed his three sons with something much greater than material wealth. He introduced them to the gifts of faith, hard work, and a love for the infinite variety of life. Above all, he imparted a sense of unity that would hold them together like the string around the bundle of sticks. Over the years, the Pitcairn family has taken pride in doing things together.

At the same time, with a policy of voluntary association at our family office, we were faced with the challenge of keeping our family unity intact. The "glue" that keeps the Pitcairn family together has always been our considerable shared social, religious, and community values. We had to find a way to continue Pitcairn Trust Company's outstanding service to the family clients who remained in the family office, while not alienating those family members who opted to leave. After all, many of us still live in the same Bryn Athyn community just north of Philadelphia, Pennsylvania, where my great-grandfather set down our roots in the 1890s. We continue to do things together as a family, deriving great benefit from networking through our local community, school, and church. This effort gives us a sense of pride in being part of the extended Pitcairn family in the third, fourth, fifth, and now the sixth generations.

Re-Examining the Family Business

Free association also gave us an opportunity to examine how we conducted the family business in Pitcairn Trust Company. We felt the strong need to develop a mission statement and a governance structure that would carry us well into the next century. To start the process, we hired a consultant to facilitate a discussion engaging over 90 family members. The key family business issues coming out of this open forum were:

- Trustee control

- Succession of family members in the capacity of family trustees

- The role of family directors

- Family representation in the election process for the family board

- A written description of the key duties of senior officers of the corporation

- Maintenance of an ongoing free association policy

We identified twelve family members to address these issues. They put together a seven-page family mission and principles booklet, and they developed a written governance document to address all of the key concerns.

As a result, we now have the family elect a board of twelve family directors who in turn elect four non-family directors to bring additional special talent to the board. I believe that our current board of directors is unique in that it is comprised of third, fourth, and fifth generation Pitcairns.

The Pitcairn mission is: To provide quality integrated financial services and to achieve superior investment returns.

Pitcairn's principles were defined as:

- concern for Pitcairn family values

- high standards of ethics and integrity

- client oriented

- professionally managed team with entrepreneurial spirit

To facilitate a more democratic voting structure for the family, we developed the novel concept of "beneficial interest" that gives the income beneficiaries of the trusts an ability to have their needs and preferences reflected to their trustees.

This solution has had a dramatic impact on improving family relationships. We have put together a process that keeps family members informed, engages them, and asks them for their input on specific issues, including representation on the governance board.

Providing for the Orderly Succession

An auxiliary board of third, fourth, and fifth generation Pitcairns is a training ground for future family business trustees and directors.

We have institutionalized the issues surrounding the success needs of our family enterprise in at least three ways. First, the family trustees had the foresight in 1980 to recognize the critical need for a training and education program focused on the next generation.

Eventually, the concept of an auxiliary board—akin to a junior varsity training ground—evolved. As a result, a large number of the fourth generation of family members participated in creating a governance structure and implementing an election process that works for an ever-expanding shareholder base.

We believe that effective communication is essential for a dynamic and complex family business structure, and our auxiliary board is a marvelous tool that promotes family participation. The role of the auxiliary board has expanded postfree association. These family members are charged with identifying family concerns, recommending resources and expertise for educating the family on how best to deal with business issues, and undertaking special projects under the direction of the board of directors. In addition, the auxiliary board coordinates regular clan gatherings, many of them for fun, to maintain family cohesion.

Second, we looked for ways to sensitize the youngest generations before they came into their wealth. Expanding on the concept of an education programmed for succeeding board members, Pitcairn Trust Company developed a Summer Orientation Program where members of upcoming generations spend the better part of a week learning how to be responsible inheritors and eventual stewards of the family's wealth. We have conducted these summer institutes for the past fifteen years with great success. And we are very encouraged by the enthusiasm for learning demonstrated by young members of both our Pitcairn families and our other clients' families.

Third, we recognized that family businesses need to commit their business policies to writing. Too often family businesses are run by "unwritten rules." This promotes dissension and it fights against the trust and confidence needed for a successful family enterprise. So our family governance document goes into great detail to describe who is doing what, for how long, and how their successors are chosen.

The benefits once seen by the founders of the Pitcairn family office are still being realized by the third, fourth, fifth, and sixth generations of the Pitcairn family. The success of the Pitcairn family mission is not measured in years or even in a single lifetime. It is measured over the generations. And it continues to this day with our family preserving family as well as the family business.

History shows how difficult it is for family businesses to maintain family cohesion; however, with good will, a willingness to leave individuals in freedom, and an organization that is committed to flexibility, I believe the many benefits of family unity may be preserved within the family business.

The Pitcairn family has retained its mutually beneficial unity through shared values, effective communications training, and clearly defined business policies.

INHERITANCE IS A PROCESS, NOT AN EVENT

When analyzing inheritances and the best way to give to following generations, it is important to ask lots of good questions, like those listed below with answers in parenthesis. I give specific answers but, of course, there are always more than one answer to these questions.

1. What are the basic guidelines for parents considering inheritance?

    (Read the remainder of this chapter.)

2. When should people inherit?

    (Serially, from eighteen to thirty-five.)

3. How much is too much?

    ($25 million at age eighteen.)

4. Are there pros and cons to trusts?

    (Yes, there are many.)

5. Should trusts have restrictions based on irresponsible behavior?

    (Probably not.)

6. Can trustees serve as mentors?

    (I am, so…yes! Absolutely!)

These are great questions, but they are very specific. The theme I would like to convey is that inheritance is a *process*, not an *event*. Certainly, much of inheritance is about quantity and timing. But these questions leave out the background of the process, and the heart that goes along with it.

When was the last time you heard someone sit down to contemplate their inheritance plan and say, "I want to leave this money so that my heirs can be burdened and miserable?" Probably never. But without thoughtful planning, misery is often the result. Let's look at the complex issues surrounding inheritance in three parts:

1. General Observations

2. Myths and Realities

3. Inheritance Plan Process

GENERAL OBSERVATIONS

The right question is "How?"

As a family member of inherited wealth, and as an advisor to individuals and families of wealth, I often get two questions:

1. How much should I leave my heirs?

2. When should my heirs have control and access to their inheritance?

Although I'd like to give a quantifiable answer, a "quick fix," the fact is there isn't really any single dollar amount or specific timing for inheritance that has been proven to be more successful than any other. The answer to these important questions relates to *how to give* rather than *how much to give.*

SUCCESSION

One of the most critical aspects of inheritance is including the process of succession planning. Succession is a normal part of the inheritance cycle. It is as predictable as death, and yet, it is hardly any easier to talk about it. Inheritance involves both money and death—two topics people often avoid.

Popular books on leadership tout succession as the final test of a true leader. Planning for succession of your wealth is equally important. Recognizing that the issue of inheritance is a loaded topic is helpful; it can go well or poorly, depending on the clarity, care, and time committed to developing a thorough plan for this event.

Too often, communication with the inheritors focuses on the tactical and technical issues rather than the strategic and human elements. However, for the technical aspects of an inheritance process to be effective, it needs the context of a thoughtful and clearly defined *emotional* base.

MYTHS AND REALITIES

We all know the power that stories can play in conveying important messages. Likewise, family sayings and the emotions they conjure up have a profound effect on the lives of inheritors.

One of the benefits of family sayings is they allow clear messages about the family's background, goals, and values to be appreciated over the generations. However, these sayings can also be confusing to the inheritors if their meaning and relevance are not discussed. Here are several family sayings that illustrate this point.

I want you to handle your inheritance responsibly.

How often have we heard this one used? What's behind this statement? *I thought this inheritance was a gift. You say you want me to handle it "responsibly." What does "responsibly" mean?* The grantor of the inheritance must remove the mystery behind this thought. What's responsible to one person may be irresponsible to another. This is a wonderful opportunity for dialogue about what it means to be a good steward and to share expectations about philanthropy.

You are fortunate to be in this position of wealth. Now, be grateful.

This statement does not sound very empathetic or sensitive to someone who may be struggling with the issues of wealth or feeling isolated as a result of an inheritance. *Is this really a gift? Aren't gifts supposed to be freely given and freely received?* A more positive way would be to acknowledge that inheritance does create distinctions between individuals and their peers, but it is a gift, and it has the potential for good. A grantor should create an environment that promotes a sense of pride in the family and its financial success.

No matter what, never sell the farm.

Whether it is a farm, the business, or trust and partnership assets, the inheritor is getting heavy messages. Rigid conditions make life difficult for the family members carrying the responsibility, especially when they have to make decisions about a shared family asset. I don't think it is fair to say, "Never sell the farm," unless the farm has a substantial endowment. Grantors should think long and hard before they use such restrictive and inflexible language. "Never" is a long, long time.

Why do you use trusts if you trust us?

This common saying conveys a great deal about the way a trust can be viewed by an unsophisticated family beneficiary. The idea is complex if not confounding: *You are a recipient of an estate-planning program, with trusts being the vehicle, but you have to answer to a trustee, and your beneficiary position is most often split by the income beneficiaries' interests and the remainderman issue. So, although this trust was set up for you, it presents complications and restrictions that make it feel like it's not really yours.*

You can address these complexities by incorporating a more trusting environment. For example, you can establish some liquidity separate from the trust instrument that will give the inheritor flexibility for planning their mission and lifestyle.

Fair does not necessarily mean equal.

"Daddy always told me that I could have the mountain house."

"Daddy told them that? Why didn't Daddy tell me that?"

Whenever judgment about the grantor's intent is brought to bear, the potential for misunderstanding exists. It's easier to achieve parity and avoid misunderstanding when you are splitting up financial assets than when you are talking about tangible assets. Family heirlooms, jewelry, furniture, and real estate are more difficult because they have a lot of emotion attached to them. This will create hard feelings between family members unless there is a clear message explaining why that intent accompanies the transferring of tangible items to future generations.

Comparisons are odious.

When inheritors compare their balance sheets and tangible items with what their siblings and the children of their siblings receive, the result is unbelievable conflict and bad feelings between generations. These comparisons are potentially the worst aspect of inheritance. Avoid them at all costs! A clear statement by the grantor can go a long way in setting the tone for the way the family deals with each other.

I would like to view this wealth, or this inheritance, as an amplifier.

Wealth, by itself, has no way of knowing whether it should be positive or negative. It is how inheritors integrate wealth into their lives that gives it the potential to be positive or negative. It's always challenging.

We all know what an amplifier does. It makes things louder and bigger; it intensifies and enhances things. But it needs an input source to perform its function. In the following diagram, the inheritor is the source. Think of wealth as amplifying the innate qualities of that person, the positive aspects as well as the challenges the inheritor will face.

KEY ELEMENTS OF A FULLY DEVELOPED INHERITANCE MODEL

A well-integrated plan is a lifelong process. You get more than one chance. To create an inheritance plan that works, the family needs to come together in a journey committed to sharing and learning.

Memorializing the Family Legacy

The journey's goal is to help the inheritor have the best possible relationship with their wealth. The family legacy and source of wealth should be shared, understood, appreciated, and chronicled. It can be preserved in a written document and even videotaped for future generations to appreciate. Crafting a family mission statement as the overarching framework for an inheritance plan is also a great idea.

Family members need to recognize that love, power, trust, and influence, as well as money, are all involved in successful inheritance plans. The process should be tremendously flexible and include plenty of individual discretion. Wherever possible, encourage adult behavior in inheritors. Avoid ruling from the grave.

It's a Gift

Remember that inheritance is a gift. It has to be received. It is not to be expected. This is an opportunity for the family to talk about the role of the grantor and inheritors in choosing their attitude about wealth.

Responsible Empowerment

To be a good inheritor, you need skills, experience, and competency training to understand how wealth affects you and your family. An inheritance plan should provide funding for training and education along with worthwhile life experiences. Our company conducts a summer-orientation program for our eighteen- to twenty-five-year-old clients called "The Journey to Prosperity." We require attendance before these young people apply for summer internships in the family business.

We can expect that the typical thirty-year-old would have more world-ly knowledge about finances than an eighteen-year-old. However, a "starter kit" for an eighteen-year-old can serve the older inheritor as well. At the other end of the spectrum, avoid plans that keep sixty-year-olds waiting for their ninety-year-old senior generations to die before they inherit. Inheritance plans with a series of installments, rather than a one shot approach, are preferable.

Creative Trust Powers

I believe inheritance systems that rely on incentives and rewards, rather than restrictions against irresponsible behavior, are more effective. Trust disposition provisions that reward the beneficiary use language that gives trustees discretionary powers for such distributions. For example, the trust could match a beneficiary's W-2 income or establish a discretionary trust pay-out based on achievement of an undergraduate or graduate degree. Other payouts could reward a beneficiary's philanthropic contributions, volunteering, and other contributions to society.

SUCCESSION CONCLUSION

I've been thinking about the information revolution and its influence on the inheritance process. Data is the lowest element, followed by information, which leads to knowledge. Wisdom comes when you apply the knowledge.

Hierarchy of Wisdom:

Data > Information > Knowledge > Wisdom

It is important to know the difference between a communication system focused on data and a process committed to fostering wisdom. In inheritance planning, the data about financial assets and trust documents is usually first given to lawyers or accountants who sit down with family members and describe what will happen. These non-family professionals use a lot of technical language to present the instruments and vehicles, but they provide little heart or sharing and no reflection on the vision.

If the goal is a wise inheritor, someone who is well integrated with their wealth, make sure your inheritance plan begins with a solid foundation. Stay focused on the family vision and values without getting too bogged down in the details or tactical elements. Focus on the shared expectations across generations by adding lots of communication, education, and training. We need to put all these processes in place so we can move from data to wisdom. To summarize this process, I look to Confucius: "You tell me once, I'll forget. You show me, I might remember. You involve me, and I'll make it my own."

KEY POINTS FOR PRESERVING FAMILY IN A FAMILY BUSINESS

1. Every time a family goes through a generational transition, coupled with a transition in its business and/or its wealth, it is Risky Business! Thanks, David Bork.

2. Because it is risky business, it can be overwhelming and stressful and mess with your ability to keep a positive attitude through times of transitions. So, remember, you either control your attitude or it controls you!

EXERCISE

1. Based on what you read above, what new ideas will you use to preserve your family business?

_____

_____

_____

_____

_____

2. What needs are not currently being met to preserve the family business and ensure a successful transition to the next generation?

_____

_____

_____

_____

_____

_____

_____

_____

_____

_____

3. What immediate action can you take as the leader of your family business to minimize or eliminate the risk in the upcoming generational transition?

_____

_____

_____

_____

_____

A Final Note
ACHIEVING YOUR VISION

"Only those who can see the invisible can achieve the impossible.
The belief in your vision holds the key to creating your destiny."

— Patrick Snow

Now that you have read this book, what are you going to do? What advice will you take and which wealth preservation strategies are you going to implement? It is time to act. You can either put this book on a shelf to collect dust, or you can implement these principles in your family business to grow and protect its wealth. You can also develop a new vision of your family business as a family enterprise to benefit your current generation and many more generations to come.

I challenge you to act! I challenge you to put a plan together, gather your team, delegate this plan's tasks to your team, and execute the plan to build, preserve, and protect your wealth.

On the lines below, jot down ten actions you will commit to taking within the next ninety days:

1. _____

2. _____

3. _____

4. _____

5. _____

6. _____

7. _____

8. _____

9. _____

10. _____

In this book, you discovered how to use wealth as an amplifier. You learned how to protect and preserve multigenerational wealth. You came to understand how to properly distribute inheritances and how to build a successful family business office. You grasped how to distill your family's foundational values and how to invest in personal and organizational development. Furthermore, you were encouraged to become a lifelong student of applying leadership. Finally, you gained a new view for defining family legacies.

When you apply the strategies, techniques, wisdom, and suggestions offered herein to both your life and your family business enterprise, I promise "your time" will have come. You will be *Preserving Multigenerational Wealth*, and you will know *How to Lead a Flourishing Family Enterprise*.

I wish you luck on your journey and all the creator's blessings on you, your family, your employees, and all those influenced and affected by your leadership and stewardship.

My final word of advice is to read, remember, and apply the wisdom in the following quote to both your family and businesses:

"Go fast, go alone. Go far, go together. Your choice!"

And finally, being from Philadelphia, I am big Eagles fan. One of my favorite players is their center, Jason Kelce, who keeps the following quote from Calvin Coolidge in his wallet:

> Nothing in this world can take the place of persistence. Talent will not; nothing is more common than unsuccessful men with talent. Genius will not; unrewarded genius is almost a proverb. Education will not; the world is full of educated derelicts. Persistence and determination alone are omnipotent. The slogan "Press On!" has solved and always will solve the problems of the human race.

Therefore, my challenge to you as I conclude this book is to "persist" on your journey to preserve your family's multigenerational wealth!

To your success....

Your friend,

RECOMMENDED RESOURCES AND NETWORKS

Aircraft Owners and Pilots Association (www.AOPA.org)

This non-profit, US based political organization advocates for aviation in general. AOPA's membership is mostly pilots in the United States.

Aviation Council of Pennsylvania (www.ACPFLY.com)

This nonprofit trade association has been representing the aviation industry in Pennsylvania since 1960. The primary mission of ACP is to improve and promote the aviation industry in Pennsylvania.

Chartered Financial Analyst Institute (www.CFAInstitute.org)

The mission and vision of the CFA Institute is to lead the investment profession globally by promoting the highest standards of ethics, education, and professional excellence for the ultimate benefit of society.

Collaboration for Flourishing Families (www.GuideStar.org)

The mission of CFF is to bring together families and professional advisors who have an interest in inspiring production at a multigenerational level and in resolving problems that get in the way of such productive activity.

Council of Foundations (www.COF.org)

Founded in 1949, this foundation is a non-profit association of leadership in grant making foundations and corporations. Its mission is to provide the opportunity, leadership, and tools needed by philanthropic organizations to expand, enhance, and sustain their ability to advance the common good.

Entrepreneur of the Year Award (www.EY.com)

The purpose of EY is to build a better working world. The insights and services it provides help to create long-term value for clients, people, and society and to build trust in the capital markets.

Family Business Magazine (www.FamilyBusinessMagazine.com)

Family Business Magazine's mission is to improve family dynamics and their businesses. Digital platforms, magazines, and events provide public and private company directors, leaders, and owners of multigenerational family businesses and C-suite executives with the knowledge and skills to be successful.

Family Business Network (www.fbn-i.org)

The mission of FBN is to offer business families a safe space to learn from, share with, and inspire each other about how to guide family involvement in the business, facilitate relationships within family, and raise awareness about the importance of family business models in society.

Family Firm Institute (www.FFI.org)

FFI's mission is to be the most influential global network of thought leaders in the field of family enterprise. It provides research-based learning opportunities and relevant tools, advisors, consultants, academics, and family enterprise members to drive success.

Global Growth Forum (www.GlobalGrowthForum.com)

The Global Growth Forum (GGF) professes growth is a visible change in thinking, business, life, and others and is brought about through our action. It is evident that growth is possible only when we think, discuss, and work together.

GuideStar (www.Guidstar.org)

This organization is a premier destination for non-profits and non-profit research to connect with other non-profits. This resource provides up-to-date information on thousands of non-profit organizations.

Hoover Institution (www.Hoover.org)

The Hoover Institution, officially The Hoover Institution on War, Revolution, and Peace, is an American public policy think tank and research institution that promotes personal and economic liberty, free enterprise, and limited government.

Inc. Magazine (www.Inc.com)

Inc. is an American business magazine founded in 1979 and based in New York City. The magazine publishes six issues per year, along with online and social media content. The magazine also produces several live and virtual events annually.

The James Madison Council of The Library of Congress
(www.LOC.gov)

The Madison Building serves both as the Library's third major structure and the nation's official memorial to James Madison, the "father" of the US Constitution and the Bill of Rights and the fourth president of the United States. That a major Library of Congress building should also become a memorial to James Madison is fitting, for the institution's debt to him is considerable. In 1783, as a member of the Continental Congress, Madison became the first sponsor of the idea of a library for Congress by proposing a list of books that would be useful to legislators, an effort that preceded by seventeen years the establishment of the Library of Congress. In 1815, Madison was president and keen observer when the library of his close personal friend and collaborator, Thomas Jefferson, became the foundation of the current Library of Congress. Like Jefferson, Madison was a man of books and an enlightened political leader who believed the power of knowledge was essential for individual liberty and democratic government.

National Association of Corporate Directors (www.nacdonline.org)

The National Association of Corporate Directors (NACD) is an independent, not-for-profit, section 501 organization founded in 1977 and headquartered in Arlington, Virginia. NACD's membership includes the entire boards of 1,700-plus corporations and several thousand individual members, for a total of 23,000-plus members.

PathNorth (www.PathNorth.com)

Founded by Doug Holladay, the aim of PathNorth is to assist business owners, CEOs, and those in comparable positions of responsibility to broaden their definitions of success. Its motto is "For leaders moving from success to significance." The very nature of modern leadership tends to isolate and disconnect, often leading to unintended consequences. PathNorth was created in response to this growing crisis, curating breakthrough peer-to-peer experiences where the exploration of what truly matters is central. PathNorth offers a "safe table" for authentic probing conversations. Aha moments are common among PathNorth members as they experience this unique community together. As with the Greeks in an earlier age, PathNorth holds that "good leaders" foster good societies, thus its focus on individual transformation and the value of role models.

The Summer Institute (www.SummerInstitute.org)

While the experience of wealth is an envied one, inheritors of wealth and their partners know that the enjoyment of it is more complex than is readily apparent. Summer Institute is a community of inheritors of wealth and their partners who create an annual personal growth program to focus on the challenges and opportunities of inherited wealth.

Vistage (www.Vistage.com)

This organization helps provide solutions to business questions. When you become a member of this organization, you learn how the Vistage CEO peer groups can solve your business challenges. Included in your membership is access to 360 member industries, business mentoring, small business coaching, and networking.

Wharton Family Forum (www.wgfa.wharton.upenn.edu)

The Wharton Global Family Alliance is a Wharton initiative that centers on a broad set of issues faced by families globally who control substantial enterprises and resources. The Wharton GFA is globally recognized as the leading institution for the creation and dissemination of knowledge and practices for multigenerational families and their businesses. The Wharton GFA seeks to foster the longevity, harmony, and prosperity of multigenerational, multi-branch families and their businesses. The Wharton GFA transcends boundaries to enable collaboration and effective communication between researchers and families for mutual benefit and for the benefit of society at large; it enables thought leadership, knowledge transfer, and the sharing of ideas and best practices among influential families; it publishes cutting edge theoretical, empirical, and field research on key issues affecting families and their businesses in a range of leading academic and practitioner outlets, and it initiates, manages, and participates in global forums and conferences.

Worth Magazine (www.Worth.com)

Worth is an American financial, wealth management, and lifestyle magazine founded in 1986 and relaunched by Sandow in 2009. The magazine addresses financial, legal, and lifestyle issues for high net worth individuals.

INSPIRATIONAL QUOTES FROM MY PEERS

Below are some quotes my friends, peers, and family live by. Note: These are not quotes by my friends, peers, or family, but rather the people I've named are inspired by the quote or quotes listed:

Tom McCullough:

"In calm seas, every ship has a good captain."

"The best time to plant a tree was twenty years ago. The second best time is today."

Steve Fluck:

"Don't be upset by the results you didn't get with the work you didn't do."

"Step out of your comfort zone and face your fears. Growth happens when you are challenged, not when you are comfortable."

"Discipline is the bridge between goals and accomplishments."

"Success isn't about how much money you make; it's about the difference you make in people's lives."

Paul Funk:

"You're braver than you believe, stronger than you seem, and smarter than you think."

— A. A. Milne

Peter Coy:

"If you are going through hell, keep going."
— Winston Churchill

"Get busy living, or get busy dying."
— *The Shawshank Redemption*

Suzanne Rowland:

"Ability may get you to the top, but it takes character to keep you there."
— John Wooden

Linda Myers:

"You must be the change you wish to see in the world."
— Gandhi

Andrew Busser:

"You learn far more from negative leadership than positive leadership because you learn how not to do it."
— General Norman Schwarzkopf

Ray Betler:

"Common sense is not common."

James Hughes:

"Professionals, doctors, ministers, academics, lawyers, provide their patients, congregants, students, and clients with knowledge and courage; it is with the provision of the latter of these, courage, that one earns one's bread."
— James E. Hughes, Sr.

Terrence O'Connor:

"Every passion has its destiny."

— Billy Mills, 1964 Tokyo 10,000-Meter Gold Medalist

Jim Brickley:

"You only have one chance to make a first impression."

John F. O'Connell, Jr.:

"One appreciates efforts but pays for results."

Jonathan P. Warner:

"Be an example to your family, spiritual, lighthearted, yet strong of character."

Joe Shott:

"The meaning of life is to find your gift. The purpose of life is to give it away."

— Pablo Picasso

RECOMMENDED READING

Allen, Michael Patrick. *The Founding Fortunes.*

Agus, David B. *The End of Illness.*

Anonymous. *The Bible.*

Bennis, Warren and Burt Nanus. *Leaders: The Strategies for Taking Charge.*

Blanchard, Ken and Sheldon Bowles. *Raving Fans: A Revolutionary Approach to Customer Service.*

Blanchard, Kenneth H. and Norman Vincent Peale. *The Power of Ethical Management: You Don't Have to Cheat to Win.*

Bork, David. *The Little Red Book of Family Business.*

Bright, Deborah. *The Pro-Achievement Principle.*

Carnegie, Dale. *How to Win Friends and Influence People.*

Carnegie, Dale. *The Leader in You.*

Childs, Walter C. *The Life and Times of John Pitcairn.*

Covey, Stephen R. *The 7 Habits of Highly Effective People.*

Covey, Stephen R. *Principle-Centered Leadership.*

Crowley, Chris. *Younger Next Year.*

Dupree, Max. *Leadership Is an Art.*

Evans, Philip and Thomas S. Wurster. *Blown to Bits: How the New Economics of Information Transforms Strategy.*

Frankenberg, Ellen. *Your Family, Inc.: Practical Tips for Building a Healthy Family Business.*

Franklin, Steven and Lynn Peters Alder. *Celebrate 100: Centenarian Secrets to Success in Business and Life.*

Goldstone, Hartley and Kathy Wiseman. *Trustworthy: New Angles on Trusts from Beneficiaries and Trustees: A Positive Story Project Showcasing Beneficiaries and Trustees.*

Hausner, Lee. *Children of Paradise: Successful Parenting for Prosperous Families.*

Hilburt-Davis, Jane and William G. Dyer. *Consulting to Family Businesses: Contracting, Assessment, and Implementation.*

Hughes, James E. *Family: The Compact Among Generations.*

Hughes, James E. *Family Wealth: Keeping It in the Family: How Family Members and Their Advisers Preserve Human, Intellectual, and Financial Assets for Generations.*

Hughes, James E. and Susan E. Massenzio. *The Cycle of the Gift: Family Wealth and Wisdom.*

Hughes, James E. et al. *Family Trusts: A Guide for Beneficiaries, Trustees, Trust Protectors, and Trust Creators.*

Kim, W. Chan and Renee Mauborgne. *Blue Ocean Strategy: How to Create Uncontested Market Space and Make the Competition Irrelevant.*

Lencioni, Patrick M. *The Five Dysfunctions of a Team: A Leadership Fable.*

Levitt, Steven D. and Stephen J. Dubner. *Freakonomics: A Rogue Economist Explores the Hidden Side of Everything.*

Majer, Kenneth. *Values-Based Leadership: A Revolutionary Approach to Business Success and Personal Prosperity.*

McCann, Greg. *Who Do Your Think You Are?: Aligning Your Character & Reputation.*

McCullough, Tom and Keith Whitaker. *Wealth of Wisdom: The Top 50 Questions Wealthy Families Ask.*

Morrell, Margot and Stephanie Capparell. *Shackleton's Way: Leadership Lessons from the Great Antarctic Explorer.*

Peck, M. Scott. *The Different Drum: Community Making and Peace.*

Peters, Nancy Austin and Thomas J. Peters with Robert H. Waterman. *In Search of Excellence: Lessons from America's Best Run Companies.*

Pine, B. Joseph and James H. Gilmore. *The Experiences Economy: Competing for Customer Time, Attention, and Money.*

Pink, Daniel H. *A Whole New Mind: Why Right-Brainers Will Rule the Future.*

Scholtes, Peter R. et al. *The Team Handbook.*

Seligman, Martin E. P. *Learned Optimism: How to Change Your Mind and Your Life.*

Thomas, Evan. *Ike's Bluff: President Eisenhower's Secret Battle to Save the World.*

Whitehead, John C. *A Life in Leadership: From D-Day to Ground Zero.*

Wilson, Richard C. *The Family Office Book.*

INDEPENDENCE HALL

SHRINE OF FREE GOVERNMENT

By RAYMOND PITCAIRN

(The following is a pamphlet written by my grandfather,
Raymond Pitcairn, about Independence Hall.)

PHILADELPHIA MCMXL

1st Printing - May, 1940

2nd Printing - June, 1940

3rd Printing - September, 1940

4th Printing - April, 1941

5th Printing - August, 1941

6th Printing - December, 1942

7th Printing - August, 1943

8th Printing - January, 1944

9th Printing - January, 1945

10th Printing - July, 1948

11th Printing - August, 1955

This is Independence Hall. This is the birthplace of American freedom. This is the shrine of American patriotism. This is the home of the Liberty Bell. This is the noblest, most eloquent, most venerated monument to Free Government on Earth today.

Walk proudly here, Americans, amid the symbols of your birthright! Greece in its glory, Rome in its grandeur, left no such heritage to the human spirit. The Pyramids of the Pharaohs, the Capitoline Hill of the Caesars, had no such noble significance. For here stands the historic structure where, in 1776, your liberty was first proclaimed; where, in 1787, government of the people, by the people, for the people was made certain and enduring.

For in historic Independence Hall were adopted the *Declaration of Independence* and the *Constitution of the United States.*

In historic Independence Hall were uttered immortal words that still echo in the hearts of men; that still inspire and exalt the cause of human liberty.

Here Richard Henry Lee, in the Virginia Resolutions, first declared that "these United Colonies are, and of right ought to be, free and independent States." Here Thomas Jefferson, in the Declaration of Independence, proclaimed that "all men are created equal."

Here Benjamin Franklin asserted that "the rulers are the servants, and the people their sovereigns."

Here the Constitutional Convention determined that "We, the people of the United States," should govern.

Here our Nation received its name; here the Founders adopted our Flag; here the Continental Congress commissioned George Washington Commanderin-Chief of the Revolutionary armies; here it received the captured British standards that signalized our epoch-making victory.

§ § § §

But these are just a few highlights of the twocenturies-old Pageant of Liberty enacted within and under the shadow of these walls.

For Independence Hall and the famous Square in which it stands were Landmarks of Liberty years before the Bell pealed out its greatest tidings. Their very origin was an expression of human freedom. Their history is a long and categorical story of the birth and growth of the American Spirit.

The Square itself was laid out as the Capitol site of a colony dedicated to religious liberty and equal justice for all. The structure was designed by Andrew Hamilton, famed colonial lawyer and patriot, who won the right of Free Speech and a Free Press for all Americans long before the first volley sounded at Lexington. Its foundations were laid in 1732—the year of George Washington's birth.

As early as 1736 Independence Hall became the meeting place of that doughty body of elected representatives—the Pennsylvania Provincial Assembly—which time after time defended the rights of the people against the arrogance of appointed Proprietary Governors; which, in 1755, asserted its refusal to "make laws by direction;" which, in June 1776, boldly offered its chambers to the Continental Congress whose own defiant Proclamation rocked an Empire.

In the spacious chambers of Independence Hall the citizens of Philadelphia, at a public meeting in 1764, formally resolved that no imposition of taxes against natural and legal rights would be allowed. In them the city's leading merchants adopted, in November 1765, the Nonimportation Resolution. In them the Signers valiantly pledged to Liberty's cause their lives, their fortunes and their sacred honor.

In them a Nation was born.

To Independence Hall and the great Square that bears its name rallied also the citizens of Provincial Pennsylvania to swell with their voices a people's cry for freedom. On that wide green sward they gathered in

1768 to assert that "The Parliament of Great Britain has reduced the people here to the level of slaves." There they met to protest against the Sugar Act and the Stamp Acts. There, in 1773, they determined that the tea-ship "Polly" must leave Philadelphia with its cargo unloaded. There, in 1774, they assembled to offer aid to the port of Boston after Parliament had ordered it closed. There, in 1775, they first heard the news of Lexington, brought to Philadelphia by Paul Revere, and publicly agreed "to associate for the purpose of defending with arms" their property, freedom and lives. There they volunteered for service in the Continental armies.

There they greeted with thunderous acclaim the first public reading of the Declaration of Independence.

Throughout that whole stirring Prelude to Freedom, the Liberty Bell played its dramatic part. From the day it first swung in the high white tower of Independence Hall, its rhythmic tolling summoned both the Legislators and the people to their meetings of protest or decision. Ominously it sounded the alarms of danger; defiantly it clanged the calls to action; joyously it pealed the Paean to Freedom that fulfilled the prophetic inscription: "Proclaim Liberty Throughout All The Land Unto All The Inhabitants Thereof."

And here it hangs enshrined . . . America's most precious relic, liberty's most honored herald, history's most stirring inspiration to all who love valor and justice and freedom.

§ § § §

In the glorious development of our Nation, as well as in its birth, this great Temple of Liberty continued its significant role.

Throughout the Revolution it remained the beacon and the symbol of Freedom—even when held by the enemy, while Washington suffered at Valley Forge through the grim winter of 1777-78. And when Liberty was won, when the Colonies were acknowledged to be Free and

Independent States, it was here that the Treaty of Peace was ratified; it was here that the Bell pealed out the glorious news.

Proclaim liberty throughout all the land unto all the inhabitants therof
Levicticus XXV: 10

Then to Independence Hall—and to its sister buildings, Congress Hall and Old City Hall, which flank it on either side—came the Founders to frame our Federal Constitution, the Congress to give that Constitution substance, and the Supreme Court to assure it permanence and protection.

For here, at Congress Hall, in historic Independence Square, our First United States Congress held its concluding session. Here Congress continued to meet from December 1790 until 1800, when the new Capital was established at Washington. Here it sat when the first three new States entered the Union, when our first National policies were enunciated, when the Bill of Rights went into effect.

Here, at Congress Hall, George Washington was inaugurated for his second term. Here he took leave of the people in his famous Farewell Address. Here John Adams took the Presidential oath. Here the young Nation was set soundly on its course.

And in the Old City Hall, on the other side of Independence Hall, the Supreme Court of the United States held its early sessions to pronounce the first of those decisions which established in law and preserved throughout our history the principles of Constitutional Government.

And through the years that followed, Independence Hall and its sister structures have continued to echo the voices and the footsteps of the Nation's great. To them have journeyed all our Presidents, as pilgrims to a shrine. Here Abraham Lincoln pledged himself anew to Freedom, in the dark days of 1861. Here Woodrow Wilson came "to feed his spirit," as America plunged into the World War.

Here the Liberty Bell for decades continued to rejoice with the people in victory and to weep with them in grief. Here, for recurrent years, it rang the Anniversary of the Declaration. Here it tolled a Nation's dirge for Washington, for Jefferson, for Adams, for Lafayette. And here, in 1835, that eloquent voice was stilled when the Bell cracked on a funeral note for Chief Justice Marshall—and thus spoke its final benediction to the Nation it had summoned into the clear, sweet air of Freedom.

Noble and enduring shrines, these historic relics! Beautiful in their simplicity, sound in their structure, they preserve through the years the memory of the strength, the valor, the calm wisdom of those who wrought within their red brick walls. To us of America they remain an unfailing source of patriotic inspiration. To all humanity they stand as earth's noblest monument to the spirit and achievements of government by the people.

And if you would know what a Free People have accomplished under the Liberty here proclaimed, then reflect upon the glorious development of America.

If you would realize what has been achieved under the Free Government here established, then remember that:

Under Our Constitution

The United States has achieved a growth in territory, in population, in resources and in influence unrivalled among nations.

Under Our Constitution

The persecuted have found Refuge ... the despairing, Faith ... the oppressed, Liberty ... the courageous, Opportunity.

Under Our Constitution

All men have attained the highest human aspiration—the right to be free, in body and in spirit. All children are assured the richest heritage possible—the right to be educated. All citizens are guaranteed the greatest power known—the right to govern themselves.

Under Our Constitution

The People rule. No man is King; no man a subject. Despotism is outlawed. The Will of the People is the Law of the Land.

And of these things Independence Hall speaks with timeless eloquence to all men and all nations that love free government.

CHRONOLOGY

In Independence Square and its historic buildings have occurred events of profound significance to the birth and development of our nation. Among them are the following:

INDEPENDENCE HALL AND SQUARE

1732—Ground broken and foundations laid for State House.

1736—State House occupied by Assembly of the Province of Pennsylvania.

1753—Liberty Bell placed in State House tower.

1755—Pennsylvania Assembly, meeting in State House, formally asserted to Parliament its refusal to "make laws by direction."

1757—Pennsylvania Assembly sent Benjamin Franklin to England to demand "redress of grievances."

1764—Citizens of Philadelphia assembled to protest Stamp Acts, and formally resolved that no imposition of taxes against natural and legal rights would be tolerated.

1765—Leading merchants of Philadelphia met to sign the Nonimportation Resolution.

1775—Second Continental Congress convened.

Continental Congress Commissioned.

George Washington Commander-in-Chief of the American forces.

First Pennsylvania quota mustered into service for Revolution.

1776—Richard Henry Lee, of Virginia, offered his famous Resolution for Independence.

July 4—Declaration of Independence adopted.

July 8—Declaration publicly read from platform in the Square.

Continental Congress created the name "The United States."

Convention met to form a new constitution for Pennsylvania.

1777—Continental Congress adopted design for first American flag.

1777-78—State House temporarily in hands of the British during their occupancy of Philadelphia.

1778—Articles of Confederation signed; fully ratified in 1781.

1781—Surrender of Lord Cornwallis at Yorktown announced in Congress.

1787—Federal convention drafted and adopted the United States Constitution.

Throughout the years that followed the formation of our Union, history continued to be enacted in Independence Hall. Within its walls have been staged patriotic demonstrations without number, as well as stirring ovations to distinguished Americans and visitors from abroad. Here, too, while the nation mourned, have lain in state the bodies of many of our departed great, including Abraham Lincoln.

CONGRESS HALL

1787-1789—Congress Hall constructed.

1790-1800—Meeting place of the United States Congress.

1793—Washington took the oath of office for his Second Term.

1796—Washington delivered his "Farewall Address."

1797—John Adams inaugurated.

1799—Death of Washington officially announced.

In the resolution offered here by John Marshall, first occurred the phrase: "First in war, first in peace, and first in the hearts of his countrymen."

OLD CITY HALL

1790-91—Building constructed.

1791-1800—Supreme Court of the United States sat and handed down its early decisions.

HISTORIC EVENTS FOR WHICH THE LIBERTY BELL WAS TOLLED

1753—Meeting of Provincial Assembly in the State House.

1764—Protest against Sugar Act.

1765—Resolutions against Stamp Act.

1766—Repeal of Stamp Act.

1773—Resolutions against landing tea.

1774—Closing of the port of Boston.

1775—First hostilities of Revolution.

1776—Public reading of the Declaration of Independence.

End of the Proprietary Government in Pennsylvania.

1781—Surrender of Cornwallis.

1783—Proclamation of Peace.

1788—Establishment of Constitution.

1799—Death of Washington.

1824—Visit of Lafayette to Independence Hall.

1826—Deaths of Thomas Jefferson and John Adams.

1832—Centennial birthday celebration for Washington.

1834—Death of Lafayette.

1835—Death of Chief Justice Marshall.

While tolling the requiem for Chief Justice Marshall the Liberty Bell cracked.

ABOUT THE AUTHOR

DIRK JUNGÉ is the retired chair of the Pitcairn Company. He previously served as chief executive officer of Pitcairn, a recognized global leader in the specialized family office marketplace. He was an innovator and leader in the family office for more than thirty years. A fourth-generation member of the Pitcairn family, Dirk was instrumental in establishing the firm as a multi-family office in 1987, and he led Pitcairn's pioneering transition to a 100 percent open architecture investment platform.

Dirk sits on a variety of corporate boards, including Paramount Resources, Ltd., and L. B. Foster. He is also a founding trustee and board member of the National Philanthropic Trust, one of the largest donor-advised funds in the world.

Dirk previously served on the boards of Abington Memorial Hospital, Academy of the New Church, the Pennypack Ecological Restoration Trust, Freeman Company, and Family Firm Institute.

Dirk is a member of the Collaboration for Family Flourishing. He is a fellow of the Family Firm Institute (FFI), and in 2014, he was a recipient of the FFI Barbara Hollander Award, recognizing his commitment and dedication to education in the field of family business. He completed FFI's Advanced Certificate in Family Business Advising. He is a past member of the 1787 Society of the National Constitution Center and a past member of the James Madison Council of the Library of Congress. In March 2014, he received PathNorth's John C. Whitehead Award given to individuals whose lives integrate meaning and contribution. In 2010, Dirk was regional finalist in the Ernst & Young Entrepreneur of the Year program.

Dirk is a consultant, author, and frequent speaker at conferences and seminars on issues related to the financial services industry, family office, family governance, and succession planning. He received the Lifetime Achievement Award at the 2016 family *Wealth Report Awards* for his leadership and dedication to the family office industry. In 2014, Family Office Exchange honored him with the Fox Founders Award recognizing him as a pioneer in the wealth management industry. In 2012, he received the Industry Leadership Award from *Family Office Review* (FOR) in recognition of his significant contributions to the family office industry, and he was also named FOR Multi-Family Office CEO of the Year.

Dirk's article "From Family Business Conflict to Family Connectedness" appeared in the August 2007 issue of *Family Business Magazine*. In addition, in 2006, he contributed a chapter to the *Handbook of Family Business and Family Business Consultation: A Global Perspective*, which explores the role of the multi-family office in a changing global economy.

Additionally, when Dirk served as chair of Pitcairn, it won the Family Wealth Report Awards as the Best Multi-Family Office and Outstanding MFO. He was also honored with FWR's Lifetime Achievement Award. In 2012, Dirk was awarded the John C. Whitehead Legacy Award.

Dirk received a BS in economics and finance from Lehigh University and holds the designation of Chartered Financial Analyst. He is considered a financial expert for board engagements.

Dirk has a great passion for the outdoors, and when he isn't spending time with his wife, children, or ten grandchildren, he can be found golfing, skiing, fishing, flying, or riding his Harley. Additionally, he enjoys video production—both being behind the camera and seeing a film brought to life bring him immense joy. He lives with his wife in a suburb of Philadelphia, Pennsylvania.

DIRK JUNGÉ
LIFETIME ACHIEVEMENT AWARD

In March 2016, Dirk Jungé was awarded the Family Wealth Awards, Lifetime Achievement Award.

Jeffrey Sonnenfeld, a professor of management at the Yale School of Management and a keen observer of CEO transitions, writes in *The Hero's Farewell* about four archetypes of transitioning CEOs: the monarch, the general, the governor, and the ambassador.

Sonnenfeld's description of the ambassador archetype aptly describes Dirk Jungé:

- They leave office quite gracefully and frequently serve as postretirement mentors. [In contrast to the other types] they provide continuity and counsel and want to assist, but no longer lead.

- They leave office firm in their leadership contribution.

- Guided by an inner sense of accomplishment and fulfillment, [they do not need] more battles to further prove their valor.

Dirk Jungé has worn many hats, including being the CEO and chair of Pitcairn Trust Company from 2006-2012, while also serving as a trustee of Pitcairn's family assets for decades. In October 2012, he stepped aside as CEO, handing the reins to Leslie Voth. He remained chair until 2019, when he retired and Leslie Voth succeeded him in that role. He remains a trustee of Pitcairn's family assets.

A few accomplishments under Dirk's leadership include:

- In 1996, he had the early vision and passion to help launch The National Philanthropic Trust, a charitable services platform that operates today with an independent board and management where he remains a board member. Beginning with Pitcairn seed capital, according to the *Chronicle of Philanthropy*, The National Philanthropic Trust is now among the top twenty-five philanthropic/grant making institutions in the United States.

- Between 2006-2008, he conceptualized and led Pitcairn's transition to "open architecture." No small operational feat. The new platform was rolled out in 2008 with Leslie Voth as president and Rick Pitcairn as CIO.

- Dirk served as a mentor to other next generation leaders (family and non-family) including Rick Pitcairn, as well as identifying and developing Leslie Voth as his CEO successor, a possibility he saw before she did.

A few descriptors might bring more color to Dirk Jungé as a man:

- A big heart—always ready to help

- Indefatigable and energetic

- Gregarious—a connector with an incredible ability to befriend others

- Fun-loving—in fact, some would say the life of the party, but...

- Equally serious and smart

- Wise and thoughtful, maintaining a long-term view

- Dedicated—as evidenced by his long stewardship and leadership through changes that required patience and steadfastness

- Selfless

Finally, Dirk Jungé is an exemplar of a family steward. He has not only served his family, but he has transferred those enduring family values to Pitcairn's clients.

Dirk's legacy to our industry, one that remains in an early stage of its evolution, is one of a visionary and builder in transitioning Pitcairn from a single-family office to a true multi-family office, a model for our industry.

ABOUT PITCAIRN
"A TRUE MULTI-FAMILY OFFICE"

LEVERAGING A TRUE FAMILY OFFICE FOR MULTIGENERATIONAL SUCCESS

Wealthy families and their advisors recognize that navigating successful transitions as well as the complexity of everyday life requires a focus on both financial and family dynamics.

Grounded in our century of experience with the world's most distinguished families, Pitcairn's proprietary Wealth Momentum® service model leverages a sophisticated Investment platform and adds critical family-focused practice areas such as Family Culture, Multi-Gen Learning, Lifestyle Management, and Decision Making and Governance.

Our approach combines the time-tested principles of family wealth with the most advanced thinking and services—to help families successfully control and complete the critical decisions and navigate the inflection points that emerge with each generation.

PITCAIRN'S WEALTH MOMENTUM® MODEL

Wealth Momentum® is Pitcairn's integrated, multispecialty family office service model. It is the first to balance the totality of both family and financial dynamics to drive better outcomes, today, and for generations.

How It Helps Families:

- Delivers excellent financial results

- Improves your family's cohesion

- Reduces family and financial friction

- Supports multiple generations for success